The Development
of Memory in Children

A Series of Books in Psychology

Editors: Richard C. Atkinson
              Gardner Lindzey
              Richard F. Thompson

The Development of Memory in Children

Second Edition

Robert Kail

Purdue University

W. H. Freeman and Company
New York

Cover photograph for paper edition © Erika Stone 1984.
Cover design by Scott Chelius.

Library of Congress Cataloging in Publication Data
Kail, Robert V.
The development of memory in children.

(A Series of books in psychology)
Bibliography: p.
Includes index.
1. Memory in children. I. Title. II. Series.
BF723.M4K34   1984   155.4'13   84-8184
ISBN 0-7167-1628-3
ISBN 0-7167-1629-1 (pbk.)

Printed in the United States of America

10 9 8 7 6 5 4 3 2 1 MP 2 1 0 8 9 8 7 6 5 4

To Matt, Ben, and E. M.

Contents

Preface

My aim in writing both the first and second editions
of this book has been to provide an overview of our
knowledge of memory development that would be
comprehensible and interesting to individuals with
limited backgrounds in psychology. When I wrote the
first edition in 1978, the volume of research was so
great that my account was, necessarily, extremely
selective. In preparing this edition, I have again been
selective. Nevertheless, I have included several new
topics, reflecting important developments in research since 1978. In Chapters 2 and 3, I discuss
research on children's strategies for learning prose. In
Chapter 4 (previously Chapter 5), I have added a section on the impact of sex-role stereotyping on memory. Chapter 5 (previously Chapter 4) contains a
much elaborated description of research on infant
memory, as well as a new section devoted to infantile
amnesia. I have expanded the description in Chapter 6 of research on memory in mentally retarded
persons. Finally, Chapter 7 is entirely new and
concerns the possible mechanisms underlying the

developmental changes described in the first six chapters.

Many people helped in the preparation of this book. Jeff Bisanz, Scott Paris, Marion Perlmutter, Gay Bisanz, Phil Carter, Lynn Liben, Barbara Pazak, and Jim Pellegrino commented on various drafts of the first edition. Jeff Bisanz, Nora Newcombe, and Scott Paris reviewed my plans for the current edition. To all these individuals, many thanks. I began this edition while teaching a seminar on memory development at the University of California, Santa Barbara; I thank the students in that course for their many critical comments and thank Susan Goldman and Jim Pellegrino for making possible my stay in Santa Barbara. I am also grateful to Ed Cornell for providing the article from the Edmonton *Journal* that appears in Chapter 2, to Toby Landis for providing examples of the sentences used in his research (described in Chapter 4), and to Carolyn Rovee-Collier for providing the photograph of her apparatus that appears in Chapter 5. I also want to thank W. Hayward Rogers, my editor at W. H. Freeman and Company, for his sustained enthusiasm and support for this project. Finally, I am indebted to my teachers—Harry Bahrick, John Hagen, and Harold Stevenson—for sharing their expertise with me.

Robert Kail
May 1984

The Development
of Memory in Children

1

Introduction

Sometime between the fourth and seventh months of life, a marvelous change occurs in the relationship between infants and their parents. Four-month-olds clearly distinguish between the human and the non-human in their environment. They will smile and babble more to a human face than to most nonhuman stimuli. However, 4-month-olds apparently do not distinguish between different human faces: They are as likely to smile at a stranger as at a parent. By 6 or 7 months, this state of affairs has changed considerably. Parents still elicit a warm smile, but strangers do not. Instead, the 6- or 7-month-old will cry as if wishing to avoid the stranger (Ainsworth, 1973). By 6 or 7 months, infants seem to *recognize* their parents as familiar and special individuals.

From infancy, we jump ahead a few years in development. Suppose that two girls, a 6- and a 9-year-old, have been invited to a skating party after school. Both are excited about the party and so are quite concerned that they remember to take their skates with them to school. However, only the older girl actually *does* anything to make sure she will take her skates. We see first that she places the skates next to her lunchbox. She also writes the word *skates* on a piece of paper and tapes the paper to the bathroom mirror. The younger girl, in contrast, fervently hopes that she will remember the skates, but does nothing to enhance her prospects of doing so.

As our last stop in this excursion through development, consider a junior high school student preparing for an exam in a history class. We see that the student is particularly attentive to passages that she has underlined in the text. Periodically, she seems to say parts of the passages to herself. Sometimes she looks away from the text entirely and tries to remember the underlined passages. As we continue to watch, we become more and more impressed with the variety and creativity of our student's efforts to prepare for the exam.

We begin with these examples because they demonstrate three important features of memory.

First, put quite simply, memory develops. As children grow older, they remember more effectively. Of course, this fact is not surprising to anyone who has worked with children. But describing these changes precisely and explaining *why* they occur are enormously complicated and challenging problems.

The second characteristic made apparent by these three examples is that memory refers to different skills. An individual's recognition of a face, for instance, seems to represent a different type of memory behavior than does preparation for an exam. Both clearly are instances of mnemonic behavior, but they just as clearly seem to represent different kinds of memory skills. The implication is that memory is not a single process or structure. Instead, *memory* is really a convenient descriptive term for a collection of cognitive processes. Memory development is a composite of change in each of several components of memory.

The third feature revealed is that memory is not an isolated intellectual skill. Rather, it is intimately involved in many of a child's intellectual and social endeavors. As Flavell (1971, p. 273) put it,

Memory is in good part just applied cognition. That is, what we call "memory processes" seem largely to be just the same old, familiar, cognitive processes, but as they are applied to a particular class of problems. In other words, memory seems mostly to be just a matter of the head doing its characteristic "thing" while coping with the specific task of storing or retrieving factual information, ideas, and other cognitive contents.

One important implication of this view is that from research on the development of memory we can gain valuable insights into more general changes in children's intellectual functioning.

In this book, we will examine growth in different domains of memory. Our goals are, first, to understand how memory changes as children develop, and, second, to understand the role of memory in more general developmental changes in cognitive functioning.

The next three chapters of the book concern the development of memory in preschoolers, school-age children, and adolescents. We begin, in Chapters 2 and 3, by looking at instances of memory that call for deliberate, conscious, and voluntary activities on the part of the child. Two of the memory problems discussed in the opening paragraphs—trying to remember the events scheduled for a particular day or preparing for an exam—are instances of this class of mnemonic activity. A major conclusion that will be reached in Chapters 2 and 3 is that much memory development reflects the child's growing understanding of the intellectual demands of memory problems and the acquisition of appropriate skills or strategies to cope with these demands.

Most of the research described in Chapters 2 and 3 shares a common characteristic: The memory tasks used in the experiments are ones in which the information to be memorized is not rich in meaning. The stimuli are likely to be strings of digits, letters, or pictures that are unrelated to one another and that do not require sophisticated understanding or knowledge for the child to remember them. In this way, the information to be remembered is thought to be equally familiar, meaningful, comprehensible, and so on (or at least approximately equal) for children of different ages. However, in recent years psychologists have realized that the developing child's increased comprehension and understanding of her world is more than something to be controlled in experiments. In fact, it is a powerful mnemonic asset worthy of study in its own right. For example, the child uses her growing knowledge to establish elaborate, meaningful relations in the information to be remembered and, as a consequence, remembers more accurately. Put simply, conceptual development will often result in memory development. The relationship between developmental advances in these two domains is the focus of Chapter 4.

In Chapter 5, we turn to the origins of memory, examining infants' memory skills. We will see that even newborns have rudimentary memory abilities and that these skills develop considerably in the first year of life. In this chapter we will also consider the phenomenon of *infantile amnesia*, the inability of adults to remember experiences that occurred early in their lives.

Throughout Chapters 2 to 5, we will be speaking of the typical 4-year-old, the typical 8-year-old, and so on. Of course, typical children exist only in the psychologist's imagination. Children of the same age differ from one another in countless ways. One distinctive and important subgroup of children are those who are mentally retarded. Typically, their retardation includes memory. Hence our goal will be to understand why retarded children often experience memory difficulties and to outline ways in which we might remedy those difficulties.

In Chapters 2 to 6, we will be concerned primarily with *describing* changes that occur in memory as children grow. In contrast, the topic of Chapter 7 will be the *mechanisms* of development. That is, we will consider why these changes in memory occur as they do. In doing so, we will address the second goal of the book: Using research on the development of memory to enhance our understanding of more general cognitive changes in children.

2

The Development
of Mnemonic Strategies

We join the Edwards family as they finish dinner. Mr. and Mrs. Edwards sit down to prepare a grocery list before going to the market. Judy, their teenage daughter, heads upstairs to begin her homework. Tonight's task is to outline a chapter from her history book. Jim, their 10-year-old son, gets his baseball glove because tomorrow his gym class will play baseball for the first time this spring. Jim decides to put the glove near the front door so that he will be sure to take it to school tomorrow morning.

This scenario, depicting the after-dinner routine of a typical family, provides three instances of the phenomenon to be described in this chapter. The activities of the different members of the Edwards family have two common characteristics. First, each person is faced with a memory problem—trying to remember (1) things to be purchased, (2) information in a textbook, or (3) the activities of the coming day. Second, each person formulates a strategy for coping with his or her memory problem. Preparing lists, making an outline, and placing the glove near the door are all instances of strategies used to minimize the likelihood that a person will forget.

In this chapter, we will examine the general course of developmental change in use of such strategies. Before proceeding, we need to clarify what is meant by the term *strategy*. To do this, let us return to the scenario, looking for the common characteristics of the activities that we have chosen to call strategies. Consider the nature of the activities: Two involve writing; the other, placing an object in a location. At the behavioral level, the first two seem to have nothing in common with the third. What this shows is that activities are called strategies not because of anything inherent in the activity but because of the reasons underlying the activity. That is, the essence of strategic behavior is that it is planful, goal-oriented behavior (Flavell, 1970). When the goal happens to be memory related, the behavior is a mnemonic strategy.

This chapter is divided into four parts. In the first, we will examine in detail developmental changes in one mnemonic—rehearsal. In the second, several other mnemonics will be examined briefly, to show that the developmental change in rehearsal typifies age-related changes in use of many mnemonics. In the third, we consider research in which the aim has been to teach students to use memory strategies. The final section will be devoted to the young child, who throughout much of the chapter will often seem to be a rather passive creature who often fails to act for her own mnemonic good. We will see that this description is not always accurate and we will provide a more flattering picture of the young child as a memorizer.

The Case of Rehearsal

The Edmonton *Journal* carried the following story on January 13, 1981:

A nine-year-old boy memorized the licence plate number on a getaway car following an armed robbery, a court was told Monday . . . The boy and his friend . . . looked in the [drug] store window and saw a man grab a 14-year-old cashier's neck. . . . After the robbery, *the boys mentally repeated the licence number until they gave it to police* (emphasis added).

Such mental repetition is referred to as *verbal rehearsal*, a strategy of repetitively naming stimuli that are to be remembered. Actually, rehearsal is not a single, well-defined strategy; instead, it refers to a class of mnemonics. The common characteristic of this class is the naming of stimuli, either overtly or covertly. Beyond this common component, rehearsal can take many forms. The simplest would be overt, repetitive naming of a single stimulus. Asked to remember the digits 9, 0, and 8, a child might simply say "9" several times, ignoring the other digits. An intermediate form would be cyclical naming of a set of stimuli: "9, 0, 8, 9, 0, 8, 9, 0, 8," and so on. The most complex might involve generating associations for a stimulus and repetitively naming both the stimuli and the associations: "*9-0-8* is my birthdate, *9-0-8* is my birthdate."

The multifaceted nature of rehearsal is particularly important from a developmental perspective, for this means that there are at least two questions of interest concerning age changes in rehearsal. The first is "At what age do we typically first detect evidence of rehearsal in its most primitive, fundamental form?" The second is "What is the pattern of developmental change from use of simple forms of rehearsal to use of the more complicated forms?"

One of the initial experiments concerning children's rehearsal, a study of Flavell, Beach, and Chinsky (1966), remains one of the most instructive in the area. Children of 5, 7, and 10 years of age were shown seven pictures. Then the experimenter pointed to a subset of two to five pictures for the child to remember. Children were asked to recall these pictures aloud, either immediately or after a delay of 15 seconds. The experimenter was trained as a lip reader and thus could determine if children were overtly rehearsing the stimuli. The results were straightforward: The percentage of children who rehearsed during either immediate or delayed recall increased from 10 percent among 5-year-olds, to 60 percent among 7-year-olds, to 85 percent among 10-year-olds. Thus, rehearsal was first seen with some regularity at approximately 7 years of age.

These developmental trends were elaborated in studies by Cuvo (1975) and by Ornstein, Naus, and their colleagues (Ornstein, Naus, and Liberty, 1975; Ornstein, Naus, and Stone, 1977). The subjects in these studies ranged from 7-year-olds to adults. They were asked to remember 18 to 20 words, each of which was presented for five seconds. Rehearsal was measured by telling subjects that if they "thought about" the words, to do so aloud.

Two findings emerged regularly. First, the overall amount of rehearsal was similar in all age groups. Where age differences did occur was in *what* was rehearsed—specifically, in the number of different words that were rehearsed after presentation of a word. With development, more distinct words were rehearsed. Young children's rehearsal was limited to mere repetition of a single word, often the one just presented. Older children and adults rehearsed several words simultaneously.

What we see from these studies, then, is that 5- and 6-year-olds seem not to rehearse at all; 7-year-olds sometimes rehearse, but when they do, it is only in a rudimentary way. From age 10 through adulthood, individuals become increasingly proficient in their rehearsal.

Once children begin to rehearse at age 7 or 8, they rehearse an increasingly large number of words as they grow older. There is, however, another way in which children's rehearsal changes with development. Adolescents become increasingly *flexible* in their rehearsal, modifying it as necessary to meet the demands of a particular memory problem. Consider additional results from the study by Ornstein, Naus, and Liberty (1975) discussed previously. In one part of this study, the 20 words to be recalled consisted of five words from each of four familiar categories. The words were presented in a random order. A useful strategy for remembering lists of this type is to rehearse the members of a category together, even though they are not presented together. Only the 13-year-olds adopted this strategy consistently; 8-year-olds never did, and 10-year-olds did so only rarely.

Even though children were told of the presence of highly familiar categories, perhaps the younger children did not realize the benefits of rehearsing category members together (a topic we will pursue in Chapter 3). Because of this possibility, a study by Cuvo (1974) is particularly interesting, for materials were used that emphasized the need for modifying the usual rehearsal pattern. The experiment was similar to those of Cuvo (1975), and Ornstein, Naus, and Liberty (1975), and Ornstein, Naus, and Stone (1977) described previously. The single difference was that subjects knew that for some words in the list they would receive 10 cents for each word recalled, but for others they would receive only 1 cent. The question of interest was whether subjects would tend to re-hearse and recall the 10-cent words more frequently than the 1-cent words. Only college students clearly differentiated the two classes of words: They both rehearsed and recalled 10-cent words twice as often as 1-cent words. Eighth-graders showed some bias toward 10-cent words, but the difference was not significant, and fifth-graders rehearsed and recalled 10- and 1-cent words at approximately the same rate.

In these results, we see the adaptive nature of adolescents' rehearsal. Children's rehearsal seems to consist of essentially a rote repetition of the words in a list. Only adolescents modify their rehearsal to fit the structure of the material to be remembered (Orn-stein, Naus, and Liberty, 1975) or to maximize their gains from the task (Cuvo, 1974).

Other Mnemonic Strategies

Prior to age 7, children typically do not rehearse (but they can be trained to do so). Beyond age 7, children rehearse spontaneously and do so with increasing proficiency and flexibility as they grow older. In this section, we will elaborate this general description of developmental change by examining other mnemon-ic strategies.

It is useful to begin by distinguishing between two general types of strategies. Some strategies are used primarily for entering or storing information in memory. The various forms of rehearsal are examples of this sort of strategy. Other strategies are designed to aid in the recovery or retrieval of information already stored in memory. We will consider first storage strategies and then retrieval strategies in this section. [For detailed reviews of research on developmental change in use of strategies, see appropriate chapters in books by Kail and Hagen (1977), Ornstein (1978), and Pressley and Levin (1983).]

Even on simple memory tasks like remembering pictures and words, the distinction between storage and retrieval strategies is not absolute but is, instead, one of relative emphasis. For example, one reason that rehearsal—ostensibly a strategy for storing information—is an effective mnemonic is that it provides retrieval practice (Ferguson and Bray, 1976). These shades of gray become especially evident when one moves from strategies used to learn small sets of pictures or words to strategies for learning lengthy, detailed passages like those encountered in textbooks. In such instances, the storage-retrieval distinction is not as useful; we will simply examine "study strategies" as a separate, if ill-defined, class of strategies.

Storage Strategies

Judy, the teenager in the scenario at the beginning of the chapter, was outlining a chapter to prepare for an exam. Judy is not unusual in her use of outlining as a strategy for storing information. Many students use it, and justifiably so, for outlining is based on the sound principle that well-organized information is learned more readily and remembered longer than information that is not well organized (e.g., Bower, Clark, Lesgold, and Winzenz, 1969).

Developmental changes paralleling those seen in

rehearsal are found in the use of organization-based strategies such as outlining. A study by Moely, Olson, Halwes, and Flavell (1969) is illustrative. Children ranging in age from 5 to 11 were shown a collection of pictures. Included were several animals, pieces of furniture, vehicles, and articles of clothing. Pictures were arranged in a circle, with no pictures from the same category adjacent. Children were told that they should study the pictures so that later they could say their names back to the experimenter. The experimenter said that she would leave for a few minutes to allow the children to study, during which time the children could move the pictures or do anything that would help them remember the pictures.

Of interest was the extent to which children placed together pictures that depicted members of the same category. A measure was created that reflected the number of times two pictures from the same category were placed next to each other relative to the possible number of such adjacent placements. A score of 0 indicated no grouping, and 1 reflected perfect organization. From the data shown in Figure 2-1, it is evident that only 10- and 11-year-olds spontaneously categorized stimuli as a mnemonic to help them remember; young children rarely categorized.

Moely et al.'s (1969) findings fit the general developmental trends found in use of rehearsal. Young children (i.e., 5- and 6-year-olds) did not use the grouping strategy well, but older children (i.e., 10- and 11-year-olds) did. The single inconsistency is the age at which the strategies are first detected—approximately age 7 for rehearsal and 9 or 10 for grouping. This is not surprising, for we should not expect children to acquire and master all strategies at precisely the same age. Strategies differ in their complexity, and presumably children will first become proficient

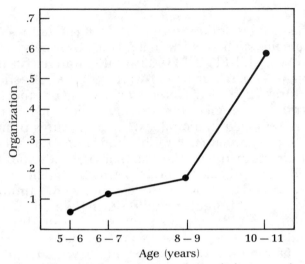

Figure 2-1 Amount of organization of stimuli during study, as a function of age. [Data from Moely, Olson, Halwes, and Flavell (1969).]

at the simpler mnemonics and will then tackle the more complicated ones.

Thus far, our picture of strategic development has been derived entirely from *laboratory* studies of memory. Is the same pattern of developmental change seen in children's real-world efforts to remember? Data from a study by Kreutzer, Leonard, and Flavell (1975) suggest that as children grow older, they become increasingly facile at dealing with the memory problems that they encounter in their daily lives. In this study, children from kindergarten and grades 1, 3, and 5 were questioned regarding different aspects of memory. Children's answers to two of these questions are relevant to the present discussion.

One question concerned how children would cope with the problem of remembering to attend a birthday party for a friend. Many aspects of children's answers showed developmental changes in study strategies similar to those discussed earlier. One simple way in which the age groups differed was in the number of ways they suggested of trying to remember the birthday party: The older children were considerably more resourceful, suggesting an average of 2.5 ways of remembering the party compared to 1.35 for the kindergarten children. In a similar question, children were asked how they would remember to attend a skating party. Here, too, there were age differences in the total number of strategies suggested, ranging from 0.85 for kindergartners to 2.95 for fifth-graders.

The nature of developmental change is demonstrated more clearly, however, when we examine changes in the use of specific strategies (see Figure 2-2). One straightforward way to remember the party would be to use one's skates as a reminder, perhaps by placing them near one's school bag. This approach was mentioned by only 40 percent of the kindergartners but by 75 percent of the fifth-graders. Another strategy would be to use a note—an idea suggested by only 20 percent of the kindergartners but by nearly all the older children.

One point to be emphasized as we consider Kreutzer, Leonard, and Flavell's (1975) results is that the children were only *asked* what they would do, rather than having been observed to see what they would actually have done when confronted with a given memory problem. This may lead us to underestimate younger children's resourcefulness, for they may have had several mnemonic schemes in mind that they were unable to express verbally to the experimenter.

These interviews may also lead us to overesti-

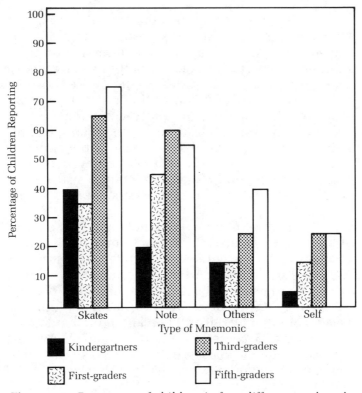

Figure 2-2   *Percentage of children in four different grades who reported the use of four different types of mnemonics.* [*Data from Kreutzer, Leonard, and Flavell (1975).*]

mate older children's sophistication. One fifth-grade boy reported that he would

Write a note, and stick it in my pocket. Cause usually when I sit down, I don't usually have a piece of paper, then I usually look in my back pockets. And then I'd go to bed, then I'd read the note, then it would be laying right there on my dresser when I got up in the morning. I'd wonder what the piece of paper was, then I'd read it. (Kreutzer, Leonard, and Flavell, 1975, p. 29)

I admire this boy's cleverness, but at the same time, I wonder if he *really* devises such elaborate mnemonics routinely!

With these words of caution in mind, we should consider another aspect of the data in Figure 2-2 that is potentially quite important. Notice that, *at all ages*, the dominant strategy is to rely upon some external device—the skates, a note, another person—to remember. Even among the fifth-graders, only 25 percent of the children reported that they would use internal mnemonics, such as "deliberately thinking about the skates the night before" (Kreutzer, Leonard, and Flavell, 1975, p. 26). Thus, children's methods of trying to remember the upcoming skating party demonstrate that laboratory studies of memory may have led us to place too much emphasis on internal, "in the head" mnemonics. Much of Kreutzer, Leonard, and Flavell's (1975) data (only a small portion of which has been included here) suggests that external mnemonics play a much greater role in children's attempts to remember than we had previously given them credit for. I do not mean to contrast internal and external mnemonics, for, as Flavell and Wellman (1977, p. 6) point out, "In real, everyday, extralaboratory life our search and 'retrieval' activities often alternate unpredictably between the inner and the outer world." Instead, it becomes apparent from the study by Kreutzer, Leonard, and Flavell (1975) that our knowledge of developmental change in memory strategies will be complete only when we are comparably knowledgeable regarding children's use of external mnemonics and the interplay between external mnemonics and internal memory processes.

Retrieval Strategies

Strategies for retrieving information are just as numerous and diverse as those for storing information, but they do share some common characteristics. Flavell and Wellman (1977, p. 20, emphasis in original) put it this way:

The individual's retrieval activities have something of the quality of a Sherlock Holmes tour de force at their most intricate and sophisticated levels (cf. Lindsay and Norman, 1972). Whether the object of his search (X) is in memory, in the external world, or both, the retriever tries to zero in on it by skillfully integrating specific memories, general knowledge, and logical reasoning. When he realizes that X probably will not come to mind by just sitting and waiting (the latter is always a good *first* move), he deliberately searches his memory for related data, in hopes that something recalled will bring him closer to X. In the most elaborate cases of this sort of intelligent, highly indirect, and circumlocutious retrieving, the process is virtually one of rational reconstruction of "what must have been," in light of remembered data, general knowledge, and logical reasoning.

Much of the available research has focused on use of category information to guide retrieval. Children are asked to remember a set of words or pictures that represent several instances from each of a few common categories. For example, children might be asked to remember *dog, table, car, cow, truck, bed, train, chair, elephant*. An effective strategy for retrieving words from lists like these is to first generate one of the category names (e.g., *animals*) and, second, try to recall all of the words presented from this category. This process is repeated for each of the categories in the list.

An investigation of children's use of this strategy was reported by Kobasigawa (1974), who studied 6-, 8-, and 11-year-olds. The stimuli were 24 pictures, three from each of eight common categories. A procedure was devised to ensure that children knew that the pictures were from categories and to minimize age differences in the way information was initially stored in memory. All the pictures from a category (e.g., monkey, camel, bear) were placed with a larger picture that was associated with the category label (e.g., a zoo with three empty cages). The experimenter emphasized that the smaller pictures "go with" the larger picture but that the child only had to remember the smaller pictures. After all of the pictures had been shown in this manner, recall was tested in several different ways. Relevant here is a condition in which children were given the large pictures and told that these could be used to help remember the smaller pictures. No additional instructions were provided regarding how children might use the large pictures.

There were several findings of interest. First, the percentage of children who spontaneously used the pictures increased from 33 percent among 6-year-olds, to 75 percent among 8-year-olds, to more than 90 percent among 11-year-olds. By age 8, children regularly tried to use the category search strategy. Second, considering only those children from each age group who actually used the cues, the strategy was used more efficiently with development, as evidenced by the average number of words recalled (11, 16.2, and 19.7 for 6-, 8-, and 11-year-olds, respectively). A third finding clarifies this developmental difference in efficiency. All 6-year-olds and the majority of the 8-year-olds used the cue to recall only one picture, then went on to the next cue. They might, for example, use the zoo to recall the bear, the fruit stand

to recall banana, and so on. The 11-year-olds, in contrast, tended to search each category extensively (recalling an average of 2.5 words) before going on to the
next category.

This configuration of results conforms to the now
familiar pattern: Six-year-olds are unlikely to use
strategies, but 11-year-olds do so with a level of expertise that approximates that of an adult. Of particular interest in Kobasigawa's (1974) data are the findings for 8-year-olds. These children clearly knew the
virtue of using category labels to guide retrieval: 75
percent elected to use the cue cards. Yet their execu-
tion of the category search strategy was amateurish. In
other words, they had mastered one part of the category retrieval strategy but not the other.

Evidence that converges on this conclusion
comes from research by Hall, Murphy, Humphreys,
and Wilson (1979). In this experiment, children were
asked to recall a list of words. For those words not
recalled, different types of cues were provided. To
understand the logic behind these cues, we need to
consider the *word association task*. In this task, individuals are presented a word and are asked to respond with the "first thing that comes to mind." For
example, when *sit* is presented in this manner to 6-
and 7-year-olds, approximately 35 percent will respond with *down*, 15 percent will say *chair*, and 6
percent will say *stand*. The remaining 44 percent
respond with such idiosyncratic responses as *bit*, *cat*,
and *throw up*.

Hall et al. (1979) selected their word list, as well
as the cues, from word association norms for children. For example, *chair* was one of the words to be
remembered; its cue was *table*. According to the word
association norms, *chair* is the most frequent response to *table*.

The critical finding of this research was that the percentage of words recalled in response to the cue for the 7- and 8-year-olds matched the percentage of times the cue elicited the target word in the word association norms. In the word association norms, the eight cues elicited the words presented in the memory task approximately 30 percent of the time. As cues in the memory task, these words resulted in recall of 33 percent of the words. It seems as though the younger children, when presented the cue, simply generated an association (i.e., the first thing that came to mind), then decided if that association had been presented in the memory task. For approximately one third of the younger children, the association *had* been presented, and therefore they recalled it accurately. The remaining 7- and 8-year-olds apparently generated a response that had not appeared in the memory list, and therefore retrieval failed.

Contrast this with the actions of the 10- and 11-year-olds. In the word association norms, the cues elicited the words to be remembered 31 percent of the time; as cues in the memory task, they resulted in recall of 52 percent of the words. These children, like the 7- and 8-year-olds, presumably generated a response to the cue, then decided if that response was part of the list to be remembered. The difference between the two groups of children is that when the first association was *not* one of the words to be remembered, the older children did not stop their efforts to retrieve. They were more likely to continue to generate other associations until they found one that had been presented. Given the cue *sit*, a 7-year-old might think of *down*, decide that it had not been presented, and stop there. An 11-year-old would, instead, generate *down*, then *stand*, and finally *chair*, the word actually presented.

These findings, then, parallel those of Kobasigawa (1974) in suggesting that one difference in internal retrieval concerns the *depth* or *exhaustiveness* with which children search. Young children respond to cues associatively, and they are likely to generate only a single item; older children use a cue as the starting point for an extensive search of memory.

A similar set of developmental trends emerges when children are asked to solve hypothetical retrieval problems that they might encounter in their own environment. Kreutzer, Leonard, and Flavell (1975), for example, asked children a question concerning their ability to remember when a particular event had occurred:

Suppose your friend has a dog and you ask him how old his dog is. He tells you he got his dog as a puppy one Christmas but can't remember which Christmas. What things could he do to help him remember which Christmas he got his dog? (p.36)

Nearly half of the kindergartners were unable to suggest any ways that the friend would be able to remember the age of the dog, but all fifth-graders were able to do so. Again, the nature of developmental change is seen more clearly when we look at changes in the use of particular strategies. Use of *internal mnemonics* was mentioned only rarely by kindergartners, but by about three-fourths of the fifth-graders. For example, one strategy was to think back to the gifts received for the most recent Christmas and, if the dog was not among them, to go back to the previous Christmas to try to recall the gifts that were received. This process was repeated until the appropriate Christmas had been determined. No kindergartner mentioned this approach, but 20 percent of the fifth-graders did. A similar strategy involved "trying to recall objects, events, or facts temporally associated with the receipt of the dog: most often, other presents received that same Christmas; less often, how old the friend was that year" (Kreutzer, Leonard, and Flavell, 1975, p. 37). No kindergartner and only one first-grader mentioned this tack, but nearly half of the fifth-graders outlined variations of it.

Finally, there are developmental increases in the flexibility of children's retrieval strategies that parallel changes already seen for rehearsal. Recall that young children were likely to rehearse words in their order of presentation; only adolescents were selective in their rehearsal (e.g., Cuvo, 1974). Keniston and Flavell (1979) have examined such flexibility in the use of retrieval strategies. In their study, 7-, 8-, 13-, and 20-year-olds were presented 20 letters in succession and were asked to write each one on a separate card. After the subject had written the last letter, the experimenter asked the subject to recall all of the letters that had been presented. One way to approach this request would be to try to recall the first letter presented, then the second, and so on. A much more efficient way would be to go through the alphabet mentally, trying to remember if each letter had been presented. The latter strategy is more efficient—for it guarantees that each letter will be checked—but notice that it requires the subject to use an organization for retrieval (alphabetization) that was not mentioned by the experimenter and that requires the subject to reorder stimuli.

Keniston and Flavell (1979) inferred subjects' use of such an alphabetization strategy by analyzing the extent to which subjects recalled letters in alphabetical order. They created a measure that ranged from 0, indicating no alphabetization, to 1, indicating perfect alphabetization. For example, recall of the letters *B E M R* would receive a score of 1 because the letters are ordered alphabetically, even though many intervening letters were forgotten. Average scores were .16, .26, .51, and .53 for the 7-, 8-, 13-, and 21-year-olds, respectively, indicating that not until adolescence was the alphabetization strategy used often.

Study Strategies

In studies of storage strategies, as well as retrieval strategies, young children often are pressed to cope with many routine memory problems. Older children, in comparison, seem to know that there are many paths to the solution of memory problems and come up with some that are aptly characterized as ingenious. Yet we need to be cautious in attributing a great deal of mnemonic sophistication to older children and young adolescents. After all, the research described thus far has involved sets of familiar words and pictures for which the number and complexity of appropriate strategies are limited. When asked to remember more complex "stimuli", like stories, more elaborate strategies can be invoked. Consider, for example, some of the difficulties involved in learning material from a text. With texts, unlike sets of pictures or words, literal recall of individual sentences or individual words is generally not the objective: The aim is to recall the main points or *gist* of the passage. Hence, any effective study strategy must accomplish at least two aims. First, it must distinguish the key ideas in the text from those that are relatively unimportant. Second, it must organize those key ideas in a concise format.

When dealing with complex study strategies such as these, will older children and adolescents be as proficient as they were at the storage and retrieval strategies discussed earlier? Research by Ann Brown and her colleagues has addressed this question. A study by Brown and Smiley (1978) is illustrative. Subjects were asked to learn a passage that was approximately 400 words long. The passage was read twice to subjects, who were then asked to recall its gist. After recall was completed, subjects were given a printed copy of the passage, along with pens and note pads. They were told that they had five minutes in which to study the passage and that they could "undertake any activity they wished in order to improve their recall" (Brown and Smiley, 1978, p. 1080).

When provided additional time to study, seventh- and eighth-graders, as well as eleventh- and twelfth-graders, improved their recall. Furthermore, it was the important parts of the passage that were most likely to be recalled after study. In contrast, fifth-graders' recall did not improve at all following study. It was as if only the older subjects knew the appropriate strategies to use during the five-minute interval to learn the passage.

This conclusion is confirmed by Brown and Smiley's (1978) analysis of the actual study strategies that subjects used. Only 6 percent of the fifth-graders took notes spontaneously, compared to 12 percent and 50 percent for the junior and senior high school students. Another strategy was underlining. Older subjects underlined more often than younger ones.

More important, they were most selective in what they underlined. They typically underlined key passages, rarely selecting minor ones.

The Brown and Smiley (1978) study indicates that older adolescents are more likely to select key parts of a passage for further study. A more complex, but comparable pattern of developmental change is illustrated in a study by Brown and Day (1983, Experiment 1). In this study, 10-, 13-, 15-, and 18-year-olds were asked to read a 500-word passage three times. Then they were asked to write a summary of the text. Subjects were not told what constituted a "good" summary, but they were encouraged to do anything—underline, take notes, and the like—that would help them summarize the text more effectively.

Brown and Day (1983) examined developmental change in four rules of summarization: (1) deletion of parts of the text that are trivial (i.e., that deal with minute details rather than essential facts) or redundant; (2) use of a superordinate to replace a list of terms, such as *flowers* for *daisies, poppies, marigolds,* and *lilies;* (3) inclusion of the topic sentence from a paragraph in the summary; and (4) creation and inclusion of a topic sentence if a paragraph in the text does not have one.

Use of these rules by the different groups is shown in Figure 2-3. All subjects used the deletion rule effectively; that is, the summaries rarely included either trivial or redundant information. In contrast, there were large age differences in use of the three remaining rules; individuals seem to acquire proficiency using these rules gradually throughout adolescence. What these findings suggest, then, is that at all ages individuals understand that a good summary should focus on the essential rather than on

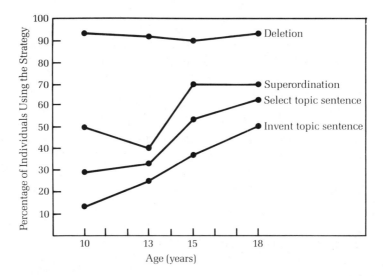

Figure 2-3 *Percentage of individuals using four different strategies for summarizing prose, as a function of age. [Data from Brown and Day (1983, Experiment 1).]*

minute details. Younger individuals, though, are less skilled at creating a summary that succinctly and effectively organizes this material.

Writing summaries may seem remote from the studies concerning memory for pictures and words with which this chapter began. Yet, underlining, taking notes, and writing summaries are all strategies for remembering large bodies of information, just as rehearsal and use of categorical relations are strategies for remembering sets of pictures or words. Furthermore, the age changes seen here are a natural extension of those discussed earlier. Recall the development of rehearsal: Children are unlikely to rehearse prior to 7 or 8 years of age; between the ages of 7 and 10, children rehearse but their rehearsal typically consists of little more than repetition of the stimuli;

beyond age 10, children begin to structure their rehearsal in a manner that takes advantage of the characteristics of stimuli. These same developmental trends were apparent in Brown's research on studying texts. At all ages some individuals were capable of employing some means to learn a text—they all used some type of strategy. However, only the older adolescents displayed the subtle and sophisticated skills necessary to break down a large volume of information into the key components that should receive priority in learning.

Teaching Mnemonic Strategies

When students use learning strategies relatively ineffectively, one immediately wonders how easily they could be taught to improve their learning skills. Many different investigators have attempted to train children of different ages to use assorted strategies (Belmont and Butterfield, 1977; Pressley and Levin, 1983). Here we will focus on the *keyword* mnemonic strategy, which is useful in learning to associate two objects or ideas. Examples would include associating a famous name with that person's accomplishment, a city with the product manufactured there, and a foreign word with its English equivalent. The keyword strategy is based upon the use of mental imagery to associate the two items in a pair. Take the case of foreign words: A student is taught to associate the foreign word with a similar sounding English word, i.e., the keyword. *Carta*—Spanish for letter—might be associated with the English word *cart*. Students are then told to form a mental image of the keyword interacting with its English translation—for example,

Figure 2-4 *A picture corresponding to a mental image that might be formed by an individual using the keyword method. Carta is Spanish for letter, so the person has imagined a letter inside a shopping cart. [From M. Pressley and J. R. Levin, Developmental constraints associated with children's use of the keyword method of foreign language vocabulary learning.* Journal of Experimental Child Psychology, *1978, 26, 359–372. Copyright 1978 by Academic Press. Reprinted by permission.]*

a letter resting inside a shopping cart (see Figure 2-4).

This strategy is quite powerful. In a study by Pressley and Levin (1978), sixth-graders taught this strategy recalled nearly twice as many foreign words as did children of comparable age and ability who were left to their own devices to learn the words. Similarly, eighth-graders who used the keyword method to learn the accomplishments of fictitious individuals learned 76 percent of the accomplishments, compared to 30 percent for students not taught the method (Shriberg, Levin, McCormick, and Pressley, 1982).

Findings such as these would seem to suggest that we can easily teach students to use more effective study strategies, with improved learning as the result. Such optimism needs to be tempered, though, by other findings. First, children in the early elementary grades often have difficulty generating keywords spontaneously; only when they are provided actual pictures of the keyword and translation in interaction does their recall exceed that of children who are not taught the keyword strategy (Pressley and Levin, 1978).

Second, children do not transfer the keyword strategy spontaneously to new learning tasks that are, in essence, identical in structure. In one study, fifth- and sixth-graders were taught to use the keyword strategy to learn the products manufactured in different cities. These students did not, however, spontaneously transfer the strategy to the formally identical task of learning the translations of Latin words. Instead, fifth- and sixth-graders needed to be told that the keyword method was appropriate for the new task as well. Furthermore, these students used the keyword method optimally only when *reinstructed* in its use with examples involving Latin words and their translations. Although high school students spontaneously transferred the keyword strategy to the task of learning Latin words, even they benefited from instructions that explicitly showed how the keyword strategy could be used in learning Latin words (Pressley and Dennis-Rounds, 1980; also O'Sullivan and Pressley, 1984).

Third, when training classrooms of students to use this technique, a number of components seem to be important. These include demonstrating the power of the keyword strategy compared to conventional learning strategies, extensive examples of keywords, and extensive practice in generating keywords (Jones and Hall, 1982; Levin, Pressley, McCormick, Miller, and Shriberg, 1979).

The collective implication of these studies, then, is that it is one thing to teach students to use a learning strategy successfully once, and it is quite another for students to use the trained strategy thereafter on new tasks. Furthermore, this conclusion is not limited to the keyword method; it probably can be generalized to efforts to train students in most learning strategies (e.g., Brown, Bransford, Ferrara, and Campione, 1983). The situation actually bears an uncanny resemblance to training circus animals: We can train students to mimic the learning activities of a teacher, just as we can teach a seal to balance a ball or a dolphin to jump through a hoop. *Intelligent* use of such a trained strategy, however, involves more than sheer mimicry; it involves understanding *why* a strategy is effective so that a student can decide when the strategy would be useful, as well as when it would yield little success. As Pressley, Borkowski, and O'Sullivan (1984) phrased it, "When learners possess an appropriate strategy together with the corresponding knowledge or information about its various uses, they stand in good position to make an 'informed' judgment about strategy deployment" (p. 8). We know much less about how to instill this appreciation of the subtleties of learning strategies. But we will return to this topic in Chapter 3.

Young Children's Use of Strategies: A Reexamination

At the beginning of this chapter, I indicated that our initial description of the "young child as strategist" would not be overly complimentary. We have since seen that young children do not rehearse, do not group material according to semantic similarity, do not use category labels to aid retrieval, and suggest few solutions for real-world memory problems. The young child seems inept indeed.

Yet somehow this characterization does not "ring true." Parents of preschoolers often report that their children remember exceptionally *well*, not poorly. In fact, preschoolers' recognition memory is remarkably effective. Brown and Scott (1971), for example, investigated 4-year-olds' short- and long-term retention of color pictures of familiar objects. A series of 100 stimuli was constructed in which 44 pictures were shown twice and 12 were shown once. Short-term retention was investigated by varying the number of pictures that intervened between the first and second presentations of a particular picture. The number of intervening pictures ranged from 0 to 25. Long-term retention was examined by retesting children after 1, 2, 7, or 28 days. To assess long-term retention, a set of 72 pictures was constructed that consisted of three types of pictures: 36 pictures that had not been shown; 24 pictures that had been tested originally and thus had been seen twice; and 12 pictures that had not been tested originally and thus had been seen only once.

Children's short-term recognition was highly accurate (averaging 98 percent) and was essentially unaffected by the number of intervening pictures. For example, when the first and second presentations of a picture were separated by 25 pictures, children recognized the picture on its second presentation with 100 percent accuracy. A different pattern of results was found in long-term retention. Pictures that were seen twice initially were recognized with near-perfect accuracy (94 percent) after a single day and with approximately 75 percent accuracy after a month. Pictures seen only once were recognized fairly accurately after one day (84 percent), somewhat accurately after a week (75 percent), but not reliably after a month (56 percent).

Parents sometimes mention behaviors that imply use of strategies by young children (Perlmutter, 1980). Consider, for example, the following conversation I had early one morning with my son, then 4 years old.

BK: *Can you remember to fix my tauntaun* and my flag?*
RK: *I'll try.*
BK: *I know how you can remember to do it.*
RK: *How?*
BK: *Write it down on a piece of paper.*

He clearly knows the value of external mnemonics. Why, then, this discrepancy between young children's infrequent use of mnemonics and what we feel they are capable of doing? One way to resolve this discrepancy is to determine why young children do not use strategies on memory tasks. In particular, it is important to determine if young children's failure to use strategies such as rehearsal reflects their *inability* to do so or if they are capable of strategic behavior but for some unknown reason do not use strategies spontaneously. One simple explanation for children's failure to rehearse would be their relative unfamiliarity with memory tasks. Perhaps if these children were given additional experience they would begin to rehearse spontaneously. Glidden (1977) examined this possibility by testing 5-year-olds' recall on five consecutive days. There was little evidence of spon-

*A snow lizard inhabiting the planet of Hoth in *The Empire Strikes Back.*

taneous rehearsal by these children at any time throughout the experiment. Furthermore, the explanation is not simply that 5- and 6-year-olds find these tasks boring and are poorly motivated to use strategies: Providing a reward for each word recalled has no impact on the likelihood that a 6-year-old will rehearse spontaneously (Gelabert, Torgesen, Dice and Murphy, 1980).

Merely providing children with additional experience or incentive is insufficient to induce them to rehearse. To determine what specific experiences are necessary, there have been several attempts to teach young children to rehearse.

The initial experiment was by Keeney, Cannizzo, and Flavell (1967). From a large number of 6- and 7-year-olds, children were identified who consistently rehearsed or who consistently failed to rehearse. In order to identify these two groups, children were tested on the delayed recall test used by Flavell, Beach, and Chinsky (1966) in which the experimenter recorded children's lip movements. Rehearsers were children for whom lip movements were detected on at least nine of ten trials; nonrehearsers were those for whom lip movements were absent on a similar number of trials. Half of the first group of children and all of the latter group were trained to rehearse. Children were told to whisper the names of the stimuli over and over until the memory test was given. Several training trials followed in which children were prompted if they failed to rehearse correctly. Several test trials were then given in which children tried to remember from two to five pictures.

Rehearsal training was highly effective. Children who had not rehearsed spontaneously at all now did

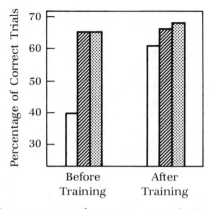

Spontaneous rehearsers—no training
Spontaneous rehearsers—training
Failed to rehearse spontaneously—training

Figure 2-5 *Percentage of trials on which all pictures were remembered accurately, as a function of rehearsal training, for 6- and 7-year-old children who rehearsed spontaneously and those who did not rehearse spontaneously. [Data from Keeney, Cannizzo, and Flavell (1967).]*

so on more than 75 percent of the test trials. Furthermore, rehearsal had a clear facilitating effect on recall. As can be seen in Figure 2-5, before training, children who did not rehearse recalled less accurately than either group of spontaneous rehearsers. After training, differences between groups were negligible. Thus, children can easily be taught to rehearse, with immediate beneficial effects on their performance.

One other intriguing finding from this study merits our attention. After the tenth recall trial following training, the experimenter explained to the children that they could continue to say the names if they wished, but that it was no longer required for them to do so. Three additional recall trials followed. During these trials, 10 of the 17 children who had failed to rehearse initially reverted completely to this nonrehearsal state. None of the spontaneous rehearsers did so. We see from this study, then, that training in memory can be very helpful to young children, although the effects may not be long-lasting. What these studies do not tell us are the circumstances under which preschoolers are likely to use strategies spontaneously. This has been the aim of a series of studies by Wellman and his colleagues.

An experiment by Wellman, Ritter, and Flavell (1975) shows that even preschool children will use simple mnemonic strategies to store information. Three-year-olds were told a story about a dog. Four identical cups were used as props to tell the story. Midway through the story, the toy dog was placed under one of the cups ("in the doghouse," according to the story). At this point, the experimenter told the children that additional props were needed to finish the story and asked them to remember the location of the dog while he left to get the necessary props. The experimenter was gone for about 40 seconds. During this time, children looked at and touched the cup where the dog was hidden more frequently than they looked at or touched any of the other identical cups. Furthermore, frequency and duration of looking and touching were associated with more accurate retention of the dog's location. In other words, young children can act strategically when the appropriate behaviors are "simple" ones, with improved recall as the result.

Sophisticated retrieval has been demonstrated in a pair of studies by Wellman, Somerville, and Haake (1979; Haake, Somerville, and Wellman, 1980). In these studies, 3- to 5-year-olds walked with an experimenter from flag to flag on a playground. At each flag, the experimenter took an object from a canvas bag to record the child's performance on the activity at that flag (e.g., a stopwatch). At the third activity, a camera was taken from the bag to photograph the child jumping in a sandbox. After photographing the child, the experimenter surreptitiously removed the camera from the bag. At the seventh activity, the experimenter told the child that this would be another good place for a photograph. Of course, the experimenter could not find the camera, having removed it previously. The child was then asked to help the experimenter find the missing camera.

The problem created by Wellman, Somerville, and Haake (1979) was essentially one of *external retrieval*. That is, the focus was on how systematically children searched the playground in their efforts to retrieve the missing camera. The most effective way of searching was to search only locations 3 to 6, for these were the only spots where the camera *could have been*, because the children had been shown the entire contents of the bag (including the camera) prior to starting and the camera was still in the bag when the experimenter took the picture at location 3. Similarly, locations 7 and 8 need not be searched because the camera was known to have been missing at these locations.

Children searched in this critical area 71 percent of the time, a value that did not differ significantly for 3-, 4-, and 5-year-olds. This can be compared to searching in control conditions in which children were simply asked to find an object that was lost prior to their arrival; here the average was significantly less, 51 percent. Note, however, that the average of 71 percent means that preschoolers are not perfectly systematic in their search. In fact, only 6 of 70 preschool-ers—all 4- and 5-year-olds—searched in all four loca-tions in the critical area and only in those locations.

These findings do not contradict the research described earlier in this chapter; they merely force us to modify our previous conclusions. Young children *can* behave strategically on memory tasks. They are most likely to do so when the tasks require memory strategies that are likely to be valuable to preschoolers in their own environments, such as strategies for find-ing lost or missing objects. Of course, the preschool-er's strategic repertoire is quite limited compared to that of the adolescent and adult. Throughout the school years, the repertoire expands to include the more powerful verbal and semantic strategies studied earlier in this chapter.

Summary

In the first two sections of this chapter, a develop-mental progression was identified consisting of (1) infrequent use of strategies among 6-year-olds, (2) a transition stage from 6 to 9 years, and (3) reasonably mature, sophisticated use of strategies beginning at about age 10, which becomes increasingly "fine-tuned" during adolescence.

The research described in the last two sections of this chapter requires that we modify these conclu-sions somewhat. Younger children are not as inept as we once thought, nor are adolescents always totally skillful. In fact, a common finding for preschoolers and adolescents was that there is often a large gap between the strategies individuals use spontaneously and the strategies they can be trained to use. Earlier I suggested that to understand this gap requires that we learn more about the individual's understanding of various strategies—*why* a particular strategy should be used, when and how it should improve recall, and so on. We turn now to these issues in Chapter 3.

3

Metamemory: Awareness, Diagnosis, and Monitoring

Judy, the teenager described at the beginning of Chapter 2, is now in her history class, about to take an exam. When Judy receives her copy of the exam, she quickly scans the pages. She is relieved to see that most of the questions are multiple choice; only a few are short answer. She is also pleased to discover that names and dates have not been emphasized. The questions seem to deal primarily with historical concepts instead. As Judy begins to answer the multiple-choice questions, we notice that some questions seem to puzzle her. After thinking about them for a few seconds, she moves on to the next question, leaving part of her answer sheet blank. We see that several minutes later she returns to these questions and fills in the blank spots on the answer sheet.

Judy's behavior in this example tells us several interesting things concerning her knowledge of memory processes. First, she apparently thinks that multiple-choice questions typically are easier than short-answer questions. Second, she believes that names and dates are usually difficult for her to remember, but concepts are not. Third, she believes that even though information cannot be remembered at a particular moment, it sometimes can be remembered after waiting for a while.

What these observations demonstrate is that the specific strategies examined in Chapter 2 really represent only the "tip of the iceberg" in terms of important mnemonic skills. The process of putting these skills into practice is not unlike the procedure followed by a physician treating an ill patient. First, the physician attempts to understand the patient's symptoms in order to formulate a *diagnosis*. Based on the diagnosis, some form of *treatment* is selected. The physician then *monitors* the patient's recovery, modifying treatment if the patient's progress is insufficient.

The sequence, diagnosis-treatment-monitoring, holds equally well for memory skills. A person's use of a specific strategy—examined in such detail in Chapter 2—only occurs after analysis of the memory task itself, analysis to determine its goals and how those goals might best be achieved. Once an appropriate strategy is selected, the task is not over; progress toward the goal should be periodically evaluated.

Only since the middle 1970s have we begun to understand the diagnostic and monitoring aspects of mnemonic skill, largely through the work of Flavell and Wellman (1977; Flavell, 1979; Wellman, 1983), Brown (1978; Brown et al., 1983), and Paris (1978; Paris and Cross, 1983). These characteristics of memory skill are often collectively referred to as *metamemory*; in this chapter we will consider three aspects of this *metamnemonic knowledge*. The first is the knowledge that "some situations call for planful memory-related exertions and some do not" (Flavell and Wellman, 1977, p. 5). In other words, we are interested in when children learn to delimit memory problems as a distinct class with a set of associated appropriate behaviors. The second domain concerns the manner in which children diagnose the objective of a memory task and select the best way to achieve that objective. Relevant here is knowledge of the factors that could potentially contribute to the difficulty or ease of memorization. One example from this category would be the individual's knowledge that multiple-choice or recognition tests usually are easier than essay or recall tests. The final area concerns a child's sensitivity to progress in a memory task. For instance, can children tell when information has been stored in memory so that additional study is unnecessary? Each of these three aspects—identification of memory problems as a distinct class, diagnosis of memory problems leading to effective mnemonic acts, and children's ability to monitor their own mnemonic activity—will be discussed in turn.

Awareness of the Need to Remember

The starting point for any deliberate mnemonic act is the realization that there is a need to remember. That is, a young child must learn that situations exist in which memorization is called for and must also learn to discriminate these situations from those which do not demand memorization. As Flavell and Wellman (1977, p. 6) put it,

Among the important things a growing person may learn is to be attuned to and responsive to those occasions when it is adaptive either to try to retrieve something right now or to prepare himself and/or his environment for effective future retrieval.

There have been many attempts to identify the age at which children first distinguish memory tasks from other cognitive tasks (see Wellman, 1977a). This turns out to be a more difficult goal than it might first appear. To see why this is true, consider the following hypothetical example. We show a series of pictures to a preschool child and ask her to remember them. Immediately she starts naming the pictures. We will probably be tempted to conclude that she is naming the stimuli in an effort to aid memory, and thus she seems to have a basic understanding of memory problems.

The problem with our analysis is that we cannot be sure that the naming was done specifically for the purpose of remembering. Young children enjoy labeling and describing pictures; our prototypic child might have done so even if we had not asked her to remember the pictures. What is needed is a method that allows us to infer the extent to which a behavior such as naming or pointing is (1) elicited primarily by the stimuli or (2) motivated by the child's goal-directed efforts at memorization. In other words, we need a procedure that allows us to judge the intentions or motives behind behaviors that appear to be mnemonically based.

An approach that meets these criteria is the "differentiation" method introduced by Appel, Cooper, McCarrell, Sims-Knight, Yussen, and Flavell (1972) and described in detail by Wellman (1977a). The essence of the method is that children are shown a set of stimuli twice, once following instructions to remember them and once under instructions that suggest no mnemonic goal (e.g., looking). To the extent that a child behaves differently in response to these instructions, we have evidence that he has some understanding of the distinctiveness of memory problems. Furthermore, if this distinction is acquired with development, we would expect that older children would definitely respond differently to the two instructions, but younger children might not. (Of course, if a child fails to behave differently, we cannot conclude that she does not distinguish memory problems, for there are many other reasons why children might behave similarly under the two instructions.)

In several studies, preschoolers have been found to behave differently—and appropriately—following instructions to remember. Yussen (1974) examined 4-year-olds' attention to an adult model following instructions (1) to remember the items that the model pointed to, or (2) that later they would play a game with the model. Attention to the model and recall of the items was greater in the first condition. Acredolo, Pick, and Olsen (1975) took 4-year-olds on brief walks through several hallways. On both walks, the experimenter dropped her keys, then picked them up. Later children were asked to locate the site where the keys had fallen. Accuracy was considerably greater when children were told before the walk that they would be asked to remember the site. Finally, recall that in the study by Wellman, Ritter, and Flavell (1975) described in Chapter 2, the experimenter told a story in which a dog is hidden under one of several identical cups. In the middle of the story, the experimenter left the room briefly on the pretext of getting additional props for the story. Children told to remember the dog's location were more likely to look at and touch the appropriate cup than children who were told only to wait with the dog.

Even very young children, then, understand that

the instruction, "remember this," is an implicit call to begin appropriate mnemonic acts. It would be premature to conclude that preschoolers have a mature concept of the subtle aspects of what it means to *remember* and *forget*. Consider these four variants of one scenario. At bedtime a boy secretly places a new book under his pillow. In the morning (1) the boy reaches for the book under the pillow, (2) the boy looks for the book on his dresser, (3) the boy's sister finds the book under the pillow, or (4) the boy's sister looks for the new book on her brother's dresser. Of these four events, the first represents legitimate remembering and the second represents legitimate forgetting. The third and fourth events, however, are not mnemonic in nature: The sister did not see her brother hide the book under his pillow, so her discovery of the book (event 3) must be based on luck or perhaps a hunch, but definitely *not* on a mnemonic basis. By parallel logic, the fourth event cannot be a legitimate instance of forgetting.

What these examples demonstrate is that successful performance on a memory task need not imply remembering, just as failure need not imply forgetting. Remembering and forgetting are implicated only when an individual has experienced some event previously and retrieves it successfully (remembering) or fails to do so (forgetting).

Wellman and Johnson (1979) studied young children's understanding of these distinguishing characteristics of remembering and forgetting. Subjects were told stories about a boy who goes to a friend's house to play:

When he gets to his friend's house he takes off his coat to hang it up in one of these two closets. But both closets look just as nice and he can't decide where to hang it. I know, you [the subject] help him. You hang his coat up in whichever one you want. The boy will stand right here and watch so he can see where his coat goes (Or: The boy goes away to play so he doesn't see where you put it). After he's played awhile, it's time to come home, so he comes back here and he says, "I want my coat, I'll look for it in this closet." (Wellman and Johnson, 1979, p. 81)

The stories were varied to correspond to the four hypothetical events described previously. That is, sometimes the boy saw his coat placed in a closet and later looked in the correct closet (remembering); sometimes he saw the coat but later chose the wrong closet (forgetting). In the other two stories, he did not see the coat placed, and he then chose correctly or incorrectly (guessing, in both instances).

After hearing such a story, children were asked a series of questions designed to probe their understanding of remembering and forgetting. For most 4-year-olds, remembering was synonymous with successful performance on the memory problem; 4-year-olds said that the child remembered his coat when he went to the correct closet, regardless of whether the child in the story saw his coat placed in a closet. The 5- and 7-year-olds, in contrast, responded accurately, attributing remembering only to correct performance based on prior experience. Surprisingly, the results for forgetting were not the same. At ages 4, 5, and 7, the most common response was to equate forgetting with the inability to find the coat. Only a handful of 7-year-olds believed that forgetting, like remembering, requires performance that is linked to relevant prior experience.

In a subsequent study, Johnson and Wellman (1980) looked at another subtle interpretation of remembering. Remembering can be viewed as a way of *knowing* that is based on past experience. Of course, many forms of knowing are not based on prior experience, as we can see from our earlier example of a boy who hides a new book. Suppose his sister finds the book successfully because she knows that her brother *always* puts new things under his pillow. Or suppose she finds it because a corner of the book is not covered. Neither example would represent guessing, nor would it represent remembering. In the first case, successful performance is based on an inference; in the second, it is based on present, not past, experience. Johnson and Wellman (1980) studied preschoolers' understanding that these latter instances represent knowledge, but not memory, using procedures similar to those of their earlier study. They created a situation in which the subject did not see an object hidden. In one case, a simple inference would reveal the object's location; in the other, it was visible after hiding. In both of these cases, when the object was found successfully, most 4- and 5-year-olds judged that this indicated successful remembering. Not until age 9 did children clearly distinguish knowledge based on present experience or inference from knowledge based exclusively on past experience.

Studies such as these indicate that young children's understanding of such "mental verbs" as remembering, forgetting, guessing, and knowing evolves gradually throughout early childhood. Preschoolers' notion of remembering is more general than that of older children and adults, for it includes forms of knowing that are not strictly based on prior experience. Not until the middle elementary years do children restrict remembering to refer to knowing that is derived from past experiences.

Diagnosis

At the beginning of this chapter, I suggested that when individuals are asked to solve a memory problem of some sort, a diagnostic phase ensues in which they try to determine the likely difficulty of achieving a mnemonic goal, and then select a strategy that would be likely to achieve that goal. Much is known about age differences in assessing the difficulty of memory goals; much less is known regarding how children select appropriate mnemonics.

Assessing Task Difficulty

The variables that can affect the difficulty of a memory task literally fill the pages of textbooks on human memory. Children's knowledge of two classes of these variables has been studied extensively. The first is the manner in which the ease of memorization may be influenced by characteristics of the stimuli to be remembered and interrelations among stimuli to be remembered. The second concerns differences in difficulty among memory responses. Differences in the ease of recalling familiar versus unfamiliar pictures would be an example of the first class; differences in the ease of recall versus recognition would be an example of the second.

Characteristics of Stimuli. Children as young as age 6 know that the familiarity of an item is an important determinant of its memorability (Kreutzer, Leonard, and Flavell, 1975). When the focus is shifted from one item to the factors that influence memorization of *sets of items*, the gaps in the young child's knowledge are numerous. Children of this age and younger know that the spatial arrangement of stimuli is typically irrelevant: Items presented close together on a table top are judged no easier to remember than those spaced apart (Kreutzer, Leonard, and Flavell, 1975). In addition, young children typically judge that the number of items is critical. Even 3- and 4-year-olds believe that a larger set of pictures will be more difficult to remember than a smaller set (Wellman, 1977b; Yussen and Bird, 1979). However, young children's understanding of quantity as a memory-relevant variable suffers a severe shortcoming. As an illustration, consider these three pairs of memory problems: (1) remembering 1 digit versus remembering 2; (2) remembering 6 digits versus 12; and (3) remembering 500 digits versus 1000. In each case, one problem involves twice as many digits as the other, but that does not mean that one problem is always twice as difficult as the other. To the contrary, the two problems in (1) are both trivial, just as the two problems in (3) are impossible, even for memory experts (e.g., Ericsson, Chase, and Faloon, 1980). Only in (2) do the problems clearly differ in difficulty.

These differences in difficulty can be traced to the notion of *immediate memory span*, defined as the number of items (usually digits) that a person can accurately recall in order. Memory span increases steadily throughout childhood, from about four or five digits for 5-year-olds, to six digits for 9-year-olds, to seven digits for adults (Dempster, 1981). The key point is that it is not the *absolute number* of digits that makes a task difficult, but the number *relative to memory span*. Tasks involving fewer items than memory span should all be solved accurately, but tasks whose items far exceed span are comparably difficult. Only when the number of items is in the vicinity of memory span does quantity become critical. Thus, a 9-year-old should judge that recalling 1 to 3 digits would be easy, for that is well within the limits of memory span. Recall of 10 or more digits should be very difficult because the quantities far exceed span. Only between (approximately) 5 and 9 digits is there a close relationship between the number of digits and the likelihood that the child will recall the entire set.

Children's understanding of the impact of immediate memory span on task difficulty was examined in two similar experiments (Flavell, Friedrichs, and Hoyt, 1970; Yussen and Levy, 1975) by asking subjects to predict the number of pictures they would be able to recall. An experimenter first briefly showed the subject a card with a single picture mounted on it. The card was then covered, and the subject was asked if she thought she could remember the picture. This procedure was repeated, except that on ensuing trials the number of pictures on the cards was increased up to a maximum of ten. After the prediction task, the child's actual memory span was assessed.

The combined data from the two experiments are shown in Figure 3-1, which depicts both predicted and actual recall as a function of grade level. It is immediately apparent from Figure 3-1 that the discrepancy between predicted and actual recall is enormous for those children who have not yet entered school. In the early school years, children become more realistic in their predictions, such that by grade 4 children estimate their recall with precision approximating that of adults. Another way of looking at these findings is to tabulate the percentage of subjects at each grade who predicted that they would be able to recall all ten pictures. The percentage of these

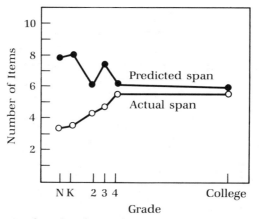

Figure 3-1 *Predicted and actual memory spans as a function of grade.* N = *nursery school children,* K = *kindergarten children.* [*Data from Flavell, Friedrichs and Hoyt (1970) and Yussen and Levy (1975).*]

"unrealistic estimators" was more than 50 percent for preschool and kindergarten children, 20–25 percent for second-, third-, and fourth-graders, and less than 5 percent for college students.

What is most striking about these findings is the complete mismatch between the two younger groups' expectations and their outcomes. These children seem totally oblivious to the limited span of immediate memory (an impression supported by some of their spontaneous comments, Yussen and Levy, 1975). Before considering the implication of this finding, we need to examine two related issues. First, perhaps these findings reflect young children's inability to predict their abilities and behavior in any context. In other words, the young child's performance may reflect not only ignorance of his memory skills but also ignorance of many of his talents and abilities. The second issue concerns the extent to which young children's erroneous beliefs about their memory spans can be made more realistic.

Findings from a study by Markman (1973) are relevant to both issues. She tested 5-year-olds' ability to predict their recall, using procedures akin to those of Flavell, Friedrichs, and Hoyt (1970). The novel aspect of her experiment was that she also tested children's ability to predict whether they could jump various distances. Children were highly inaccurate when predicting memory but were much more successful when predicting jumping. Thus the findings of Flavell, Friedrichs, and Hoyt (1970) and Yussen and Levy (1975) seem to reflect specific ignorance of memory limitations, rather than insensitivity to all skills.

Regarding the issue of the malleability of the young child's belief, Markman also found that 5-year-olds became more realistic in their predictions when their recall was tested repeatedly. Similarly, Yussen and Levy (1975) showed that children would estimate more realistically when they were told whether an "average peer" would be able to recall a card with n pictures on it. Third-graders were particularly influenced by this type of information; preschoolers were also influenced, but to a lesser extent.

What is the implication of the preschoolers' unrealistic predictions for their memory behavior? It would seem plausible that younger children's erroneous view of their memory span might lull them into a false sense of mnemonic security. In other words, if the average 4-year-old believes that she has a memory span of eight items, then she may not see the need to resort to mnemonics.

Young children do not realize that memory span can reduce the impact of quantity of information on memory difficulty. In like manner, young children apparently do not appreciate the fact that, given certain relationships among stimuli, memorization of even a lengthy list may be trivial. This point is well illustrated by a finding from Kreutzer, Leonard, and Flavell's (1975) study. Children first practiced learning to associate pairs of words in a list (e.g., *car* and *shirt*, *boat* and *apple*). After this practice, they were shown two lists and were asked to predict which would be easier to learn and remember. Pairs in one list consisted of names and actions (*Mary* and *walk*, *Anne* and *sit*); pairs in the second list consisted of highly associated antonyms (*cry* and *laugh*, *black* and *white*). The 9- and 11-year-olds were confident that the latter of the two lists was less formidable, but 6- and 7-year-olds saw no compelling reason why the lists should differ in difficulty, even though the semantic relations in the second list had been described explicitly.

Another finding from this study demonstrates the importance that 6- and 7-year-olds attach to quantity of information as a factor determining memory difficulty. After children had indicated which of the two lists would be easier to learn, the experimenter added one more pair to this "preferred list" and asked the children to reevaluate their decisions. Nearly all 6- and 7-year-olds immediately changed their minds, deciding that the previously more difficult, but now shorter, list would be easier. The older children were more confident in their original selection of the list of antonyms. Most were certain that a list of seven pairs of antonyms would still be easier than a list of four pairs of unrelated words. One child—obviously the budding mnemonist of the group—felt that a list of 50 antonyms would still be preferable to four pairs of unrelated words.

Younger children's apparent ignorance of the benefits of semantic relations is also seen in a study by Moynahan (1973). Children were asked to evaluate the relative difficulties of memorizing conceptually related versus conceptually unrelated lists of words. The 9- and 10-year-olds, like those in the Kreutzer, Leonard, and Flavell (1975) study, were confident of the mnemonic benefits of the presence of conceptual categories; younger children were less likely to be aware of these benefits.

Characteristics of Memory Tests. After a child has memorized some information, her retention can be measured in assorted ways. The measure might be one of recognition or recall. If the measure is recall, then either verbatim or paraphrased recall might be allowed. Regardless of the specific variation selected, the test could be given either immediately or after a delay of some interval. Each of these variables contributes to the difficulty of a memory problem, and each has been examined in studies of metamemory development.

Speer and Flavell (1979) told stories to kindergarten and grade 1 children in which the story characters—twin children of unspecified ages—were faced with memory problems. The problems were the same for the twins, with the exception that one twin's problem required recall, but the other's demanded recognition. For example, in one story each twin went to a neighbor to borrow ingredients to bake a cake. One neighbor asked one twin what ingredients she needed (recall); the second neighbor told the other twin to select the ingredients "from all the things in the kitchen" (recognition). Children heard pairs of stories like these and then were asked to decide which of the twins, if either, had the easier memory task.

Among 16 kindergartners, 6 consistently selected the recognition task as the easier of the two, 1 said they were of equal difficulty, and 9 were uncertain or inconsistent. Among the 16 first-graders, 9 selected the recognition task, 1 said they were equal, and 6 were uncertain. No child at either grade level consistently selected the recall task as easier. A difference between the two grades was that all 9 of the first-graders who selected the recognition task were able to justify their answers, but only 3 of the 6 kindergartners could do so. It appears, then, that the recall-recognition distinction is established in a basic form at an early age, although young children may not fully understand why recognition is easier, since they had difficulty justifying their selection.

Because young children are sensitive to the difficulty of recalling information, it is of interest to see if they also are cognizant of the mnemonic consequences of variations in the format of recall. Children's awareness of differences between verbatim and paraphrased recall was studied by Kreutzer, Leonard, and Flavell (1975) and by Myers and Paris (1978). Kreutzer, Leonard, and Flavell (1975, p. 43) told the subjects in their study this story:

The other day I played a record of a story for a girl. I asked her to listen carefully to the record as many times as she wanted so she could tell me the story later. Before she began to listen to the record, she asked me one question: "Am I supposed to remember the story word for word, just like on the record, or can I tell you in my own words?"

Myers and Paris (1978) followed a similar format, with second- and sixth-graders, but the hypothetical child was to read the story rather than listen to it. In both studies, the experimenter then asked the child several questions designed to probe her comprehension of the difference between verbatim and paraphrased recall.

One question concerned why the hypothetical child wanted to know if recall was to be verbatim or could be paraphrased. Children from kindergarten through grade 2 had great difficulty answering this question, with the vast majority either not knowing or giving an irrelevant answer. Children from the upper grades grasped the motivation for the hypothetical child's question. Most said that she needed to know because it would affect the difficulty of memorization and the way in which she would read (or listen to) the story.

Another question was intended to provide a more straightforward assessment of children's understanding: Subjects were simply asked whether verbatim or paraphrased recall was easier. The percentage of children in the two studies who selected paraphrased recall is shown in Figure 3-2. A slight majority of kindergartners understood the ease of paraphrased recall compared to verbatim recall. The percentage climbed steadily, until by grades 5 and 6 all children understood the difference.

A final aspect of metamemory regarding the difficulty of both recall and recognition tasks is the amount of time elapsed between presentation of material and the test of retention. Kreutzer, Leonard, and Flavell (1975, p. 9) asked children, "If you wanted to phone your friend and someone told you the phone number, would it make any difference if you called right away after you heard the number or if you got a drink of water first?"

At each grade level, the most frequent response was "Phone first." Furthermore, most of the children who answered in this way explained that it was necessary to call right away to minimize the likeli-

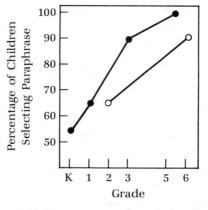

● Kreutzer, Leonard, and Flavell (1975)
○ Myers and Paris (1978)

Figure 3-2 *Percentage of children selecting paraphrase as easier than verbatim recall, as a function of grade.* K = kindergarten children. [Data from Kreutzer, Leonard, and Flavell (1975) and Myers and Paris (1978).]

hood of either forgetting the number or forgetting to make the call altogether. Comprehension of this need did develop, with approximately 60 percent of the kindergarten and grade 1 children understanding the effects of delay on retention and more than 90 percent of the third- and fifth-graders understanding them.

Interactions among Memory Variables

In the research described thus far, the focus has been on children's ability to evaluate the contribution of a single variable (e.g., quantity, gist versus verbatim recall) in determining memory difficulty. When children encounter their own memory problems, more often several variables may contribute to the difficulty of the problems. For example, in deciding how difficult it will be to remember the material in a textbook, some of the relevant variables would include the length of time allowed for study of the material, the familiarity of the material, the quantity of information, the nature of the test (and whether it is known), and so on. Furthermore, many of these variables do not operate independently. A long chapter that is familiar and interesting may be easier to learn than a shorter chapter that is boring.

Children's understanding of the way in which variables can interact to determine the difficulty of memory problems has been examined in several studies. Wellman (1978) presented children with problems in which one variable was relevant, as well as problems in which two variables were relevant. An example of a one-variable problem would be a drawing of three boys, who were depicted as trying to remember 3, 9, or 18 items. Here of course, the correct answer would be that the boy with 18 items has the most difficult task.

Illustrative of a two-variable problem would be the three drawings shown in Figure 3-3: (1) a drawing of a boy with 18 items to remember who merely looks at the items; (2) a similar boy with 3 items; and (3) a boy with 3 items to remember who writes down the names of the items. Here, (1) is the most difficult because of the quantity involved; (2) and (3) are equal in terms of quantity, but (2) should be more difficult because of differences in the boys' efforts to remember.

Wellman (1978) found that both 5- and 10-year-olds answered one-variable problems accurately (88 and 98 percent). However, 5-year-olds answered only 32 percent of the two-variable problems correctly, compared to 98 percent for the 10-year-olds. Fur-

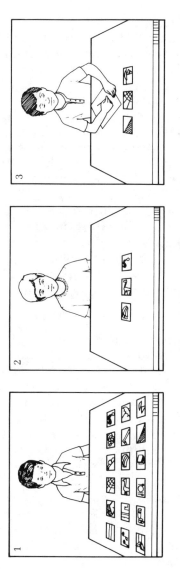

Figure 3-3 An example of a two-variable problem presented to children in the Wellman (1978) study. The boys differ in the number of items they must recall (18, 3, and 3) and their strategy for doing so (looking, looking, writing them down).

thermore, 5-year-olds' errors were quite systematic: These children judged the difficulty of problems on only one dimension. In the illustration given above, for example, they would judge that (1) is more difficult than (2) and (3), which they would judge to be equally difficult.

In a subsequent study (Wellman, Collins and Glieberman, 1981), the problems varied in terms of the number of items and the effort of the child attempting to remember the items. Subjects were asked to predict the number of items that the pictured child would recall. Here, 5-, 8-, 10-, and 19-year-olds all considered both effort and quantity in their predictions. However, young children's predictions were influenced much more by effort than by the number of items, consistent with other instances in which young children believe that sheer effort can overcome cognitive obstacles (e.g., Nicholls, 1978). Not until age 19 did subjects weigh effort and quantity approximately equally.

The findings of Wellman's two studies (1978; Wellman, Collins, and Glieberman, 1981) may seem inconsistent, for in one study young children completely ignored one of the two variables, but in the other they considered both variables (though not equally). This discrepancy is probably more apparent than real. First, different procedures were used in the two studies to assess children's estimates of the difficulty of memory problems. Second, and more important, there is no reason to expect children's understanding of interactions among memory variables to emerge, in full bloom, at some magic age. Just as children learn about the mnemonic impact of individual variables throughout the school years, so too do they gradually learn the impact of particular combinations of memory variables.

Perhaps the most sobering aspect of Wellman's work is how late subtle reasoning about memory problems develops. Not until adolescence and young adulthood do individuals evaluate the combined impact of memory variables with some precision.

Selecting Appropriate Strategies

After a child evaluates the factors involved in a memory problem and derives a rough estimate of its difficulty, he must select a memory strategy likely to achieve the mnemonic goal. This choice is presumably based upon the child's understanding of different mnemonics and of the appropriateness of a given mnemonic for a particular memory problem (e.g., rehearsal is well suited for telephone numbers but is hardly the strategy of choice for remembering the words or lines of *Othello*).

In fact, there is little evidence concerning children's *knowledge* of strategies and the match between strategies and memory problems. This is particularly surprising given the voluminous literature on children's *use* of strategies.

One of the first studies that focused on the match between strategy and problem was by Rogoff, Newcombe, and Kagan (1974). The purpose of this study was to determine if 4-, 6-, and 8-year-olds would adjust the amount of time spent studying stimuli when they knew the length of the retention interval. Children were seen three times. In the first session, they were given half of a toy and were told that they would receive the other half when they returned for the second session. The interval between sessions was either a few minutes, one day, or one week. This part of the experiment was designed to provide children with specific experience regarding the concept of a time delay as it was to be used in the study. When the child returned for the second session, he was given the promised toy and then was told that he was to remember some pictures for a period of time comparable to the delay between sessions 1 and 2. The child was allowed to look at the pictures for as long as he wanted. In the third session, recognition was measured, and a final toy was given. The relevant result was that knowledge of the retention interval affected only the 8-year-olds' looking time; 4- and 6-year-olds looked at the pictures for essentially the same amount of time, regardless of the anticipated retention interval.

Studying for a longer period, as did the 8-year-olds in the Rogoff, Newcombe, and Kagan (1974) study, is beneficial only if children spend that time using strategies appropriate to the problem at hand. Relevant here are studies by Moynahan (1978) and Lodico, Ghatala, Levin, Pressley, and Bell (1983). In these studies, the task was to learn to associate ten pairs of stimuli. Included were pairs like *airplane-couch* and *lion-mirror;* upon presentation of *airplane*, children were to respond with *couch*. On one trial, children were told that a good way to remember the items in a pair would be to say their names together aloud, repeatedly (i.e., a simple rehearsal strategy). On another trial, with ten different pairs, children were taught to use an *elaboration* strategy in which they should make the items "do something together or put them together in some way" (Moynahan, 1978, p. 259). The repetition and elaboration strategies were chosen because the first should be a much less effective mnemonic in this task than the second. And, in fact, children recalled approximately twice as many pairs using the elaboration strategy as they did using the repetition strategy.

Given the clear bias that one strategy is more effective for this task than the other, what would happen if children were asked to remember a third set of ten pairs and were told, "This time you can use any way you want to remember which things go together" (Moynahan, 1978, p. 260). Lodico et al. (1983) found that 56 percent of the 7-year-olds in their study used the less effective repetition strategy, compared to 44 percent who used the interaction strategy. Moynahan (1978) found that 58 percent of the 8-year-olds in her study and 71 percent of the 10-year-olds chose to use the more efficient strategy. Finally, in a study by Pressley, Levin, and Ghatala (1984, Experiment 5) in which the procedures were similar, 100 percent of the 12-year-olds selected the more effective strategy. These data, then, indicate a gradual but steady rise in the percentage of children using the considerably more efficient of the two strategies.

Why would the 7- and 8-year-olds not use the strategy that led to greater recall? One possibility is that children may not realize that it was the strategy they used that was responsible for the difference in performance. Children may believe that the ten pairs in one set were somehow more memorable than those in the other. Or they may attribute their greater recall to the fact that it was the first set of ten (so they were more alert) or that it was the second set (so they had more practice). In fact, in the Moynahan (1978) study, the percentage of children who attributed their greater recall to the more effective strategy was 8, 25, and 71 percent for the 6-, 8-, and 10-year-olds. Of these children, 92 percent chose to use the interaction strategy. Thus, within the restricted sample of children who understood the links between the two strategies and differences in recall, these children consistently used the more effective of the two strategies.* (Paris, Newman, and McVey, 1982, arrive at much the same conclusion using quite different procedures.)

Based on these two studies, it is undoubtedly wrong to conclude that subjects will always use the strategy that should "on paper" be most effective, even when they know that strategy. To see why this might be, consider the Moynahan (1978) study in which children were asked to try to remember all ten pairs of items. Children's actual goals may have been more modest, for as we saw earlier, 7- and 8-year-olds typically realize that ten items is beyond their immediate memory span. Suppose children decide that remembering five pairs is a reasonable aim and further suppose that the simpler of the two mnemonics results in recall of four pairs. Children may decide that this performance is acceptably close to their goal, particularly in the face of the extra effort needed for the more powerful strategy. This may explain why 8 percent of the children in Moynahan's (1978) study who knew (1) which set of ten pairs they recalled more accurately and (2) that their greater recall was due to the interactive strategy nevertheless did not use that strategy when the choice was entirely theirs.

*Moynahan (1978) also tested 6-year-olds. Surprisingly, 75 percent of these children chose to use the interaction strategy, a figure higher than that found even for 10-year-olds. This figure is difficult to interpret, however, because the 6-year-olds could not reliably indicate which strategy resulted in greater recall. It is therefore unlikely that 6-year-olds chose the interactive strategy because they saw it as the more effective mnemonic for this task.

Monitoring

Earlier I suggested that a skilled learner periodically appraises the status of information that is to be learned. That is, an individual tries to decide which information is (1) well learned, (2) will be well learned with just a bit more effort, or (3) will require substantial additional study to be well learned. If most information is in category (1), then the problem is solved and the learner can stop. If most information is in category (2), then the rational choice would be to persevere, using the same strategy until the problem is solved. If category (3) applies, then the learner may reevaluate what she is doing, with the possible outcomes including returning to the diagnostic phase to find a better strategy, continuing the current efforts futile though they may seem, or quitting altogether.

Analyzing Learning

How accurately can children monitor the extent to which they have learned something (i.e., stored it in memory)? Consider first monitoring of individual items. Here the question is "How accurately can a child distinguish information that has been learned from that which is partially known and from that which is completely unknown?" Pertinent results were described in a study by Wellman (1977c) with 6-, 7-, and 9-year-olds. Children were shown 30 pictures and were asked to name the depicted objects. The objects varied in their probable familiarity to the children: Some were highly familiar (e.g., *clown, scis-*

sors), others were somewhat unfamiliar (e.g., goggles, funnel), and still others were totally unfamiliar to children of these ages (e.g., caduceus, metronome). After the child had tried to name each picture, the experimenter selected the pictures that the child had been unable to name. These were presented again, and the child was asked if he thought he would recognize the name if he heard it. Finally, a recognition test was given in which an object was named and the child tried to pick the named object from a set of nine pictures.

Of special interest is the relation between the child's judgments about recognition and his actual recognition scores. For each picture, four outcomes are possible. A child could (1) predict recognition and actually recognize, (2) predict recognition and fail to recognize, (3) not predict recognition and recognize, and (4) not predict recognization and not recognize. Outcomes (1) and (4) demonstrate that a child accurately assessed information in long-term memory; outcomes (2) and (3) reflect inaccurate assessment. All children were able to make these judgments, but accuracy improved considerably between the ages of 6 and 9.

Subsequently, Cultice, Somerville, and Wellman (1983) modified these procedures for use with 4- and 5-year-olds. Now the stimuli were photographs of people; some were highly familiar (classmates), some were moderately familiar (children in another preschool class in the same building), and others were totally unfamiliar (children who attended other preschools). As before, the focus was the correspondence between a child's predictions about her ability to recognize a person's name and her actual recognition of that name. Both 4- and 5-year-olds distinguished names they would recognize from those they would not. Their performance was less accurate than that of the 6-year-olds in Wellman's (1977c) study, a finding that should be interpreted cautiously because names of objects were used in one study and names of people in the other.

Much the same pattern was reported in a study by Goodman and Gardiner (1981). Here the child's actual learning was measured prior to the child's judgment of what she thought she had learned. Specifically, lists of words were presented for children to memorize. After several lists had been presented and the child's recall assessed, all of the stimuli were presented individually to the child, who was asked to judge if she had recalled or forgotten each item. As in the Wellman (1977c) and Cultice, Somerville, and Wellman (1983) studies, the youngest children— here, 6-year-olds—could make these judgments with some accuracy, but accuracy increased steadily throughout the elementary years. Furthermore, using the same general approach as Goodman and Gardiner (1981), Bisanz, Vesonder, and Voss (1978) found that monitoring becomes increasingly more accurate throughout adulthood.

Presumably, by evaluating progress on each item in a set, a person can judge how well he is progressing on the set as a whole. That is, we can imagine that children somehow "average" their progress on individual items to derive an estimate of their overall progress on the task. Because there are developmental differences in the accuracy with which children judge their learning of individual items, we would expect developmental differences in accuracy of evaluating the extent to which the entire set has been learned. The ability to assess when an entire set of stimuli has been learned was studied by Flavell, Friedrichs, and Hoyt (1970). These investigators determined the memory spans of nursery school, kindergarten, grade 2, and grade 4 children. Then the children were told that they were to try to remember a set of n pictures, where n corresponded to the individual child's memory span. Children could take as much time as necessary to study the pictures. The experimenter emphasized that the children should study until they could remember all of the pictures, not just some of them. When children were ready to recall the pictures, they rang a bell to signal the experimenter to return.

Because the number of pictures to be recalled was equal to the individual's memory span, the recall task was comparably difficult for children from the different grades. Nevertheless, a pronounced developmental increase was found in the number of children who recalled the pictures perfectly. Second- and fourth-graders were quite proficient; the majority of children in these grades recalled the pictures perfectly on each of three trials. In contrast, most nursery school children were correct on only one of the three trials. Young children seem to be capable of assessing their "recall readiness" (Flavell, Friedrichs, and Hoyt, 1970), but they do so with only minimal proficiency.

Allocating Effort

Individuals presumably monitor their learning progress so that they can channel their efforts most effectively. As described earlier, one possibility is that learners may abandon their current strategy if progress is negligible. We know little about children's ability to make these sorts of decisions in the course of learning and remembering. More is known about a related form of decision-making, namely, how students allocate their efforts among the items to be learned. That is, how do students decide which items to study now and which to ignore, at least for the moment? For example, given the choice between studying information that is already known versus information that is not, it is usually sound strategy to allocate more effort to the latter information.

Masur, McIntyre, and Flavell (1973) examined this issue in first-graders, third-graders, and college students. Subjects were asked to remember a set of pictures that was 1.5 times greater than their memory span. A 45-second study period was followed by a free recall test. After recall was completed, the subject was allowed to select *half the pictures* for 45 seconds of additional study. This alternating study and recall procedure was continued for several trials. On the study trials, third-graders and college students almost always selected pictures that had not been recalled on the previous trial; first-graders picked approximately equal numbers of recalled and unrecalled pictures.

The first-graders' failure to study those items that they had not recalled is not due to an inability to remember which items they had recalled and which they had forgotten. As described earlier in this chapter, even 6- and 7-year-olds can reliably distinguish what they have recalled from what they have not (Bisanz, Vesonder, and Voss, 1978; Goodman and Gardiner, 1981; Wellman, 1977c).

Perhaps young children simply do not understand the virtues of directing effort to unlearned material. Before accepting this conclusion, we need to consider an alternative mentioned earlier concerning the difference between an experimenter's goal that the child learn all of the items versus the child's more modest goal of learning a subset of the items. From this viewpoint, young children may be more likely to select previously recalled items because they prefer to maintain goals that they have already achieved, rather than try to learn more.

We should also be cautious in attributing too much skill to third-graders, for allocating effort among a small set of pictures may be far from the most taxing of cognitive tasks. Consider the prose analog of the Masur, McIntyre, and Flavell (1973) study: Individuals study and recall a story, then are allowed to select a subset of sentences from the passage for further study (Brown, Smiley, and Lawton, 1978). Here effort must be allocated both on the basis of (1) whether the gist of the sentence is already learned and (2) whether the sentence is central to the meaning of the passage as a whole. Students in grades 5 to 12 selected the most important sentences for subsequent study (though the effect was less pronounced for fifth-graders); undergraduates, however, did not select the most important items but instead chose those in the category of "second most important." They believed that they would easily remember ideas related directly to the main theme. Therefore, they chose to study sentences that contained important, but not fundamental, material.

A Concluding Remark

Our understanding of monitoring is modest, for the relevant studies are few in number. Both analysis of what one knows and allocation of effort seem to develop gradually throughout childhood and adolescence. Yet, an important warning must be added here. All of the studies have concerned children's actions under *explicit instructions to monitor*. In research on analyzing learning, children were asked to distinguish what they knew from what they did not. Do children monitor spontaneously? The existing research provides no answers to this question. In like manner, in research on allocation of effort, children were forced to be selective in their study. Does the same selectivity occur spontaneously (i.e., when the structure of the task does not demand at least partial selectivity)? Again, the available research provides no clues. These challenging but important questions remain to be addressed in future research.

Summary

Metamemory refers collectively to (1) the awareness that a situation calls for remembering, (2) the choice of skills used to diagnose the difficulty of a memory task, and (3) monitoring of the impact of that choice on progress toward a memory goal.

In the first of these three categories, I described research indicating that even preschoolers are typically aware of the need to remember. However, detailed understanding of remembering as knowledge based on past experience does not appear until the middle elementary years.

Concerning diagnosis, most of the research has focused on children's understanding of the variables that contribute to the difficulty of memory problems. Preschoolers know that quantity of information is an important determinant of memory difficulty; not until middle childhood do children realize that quantity is important relative to memory span and that semantic relations modulate the impact of quantity of information. Also during the elementary school years, children show growing awareness of differences between memory tasks (e.g., recall versus recognition) and greater ability to choose appropriate strategies for a task.

Monitoring refers to the ability to assess what one knows and to allocate future effort based on that assessment. Even preschoolers are capable of reflecting on their own prior learning, but doing so with precision is a gradual developmental phenomenon. Acting on the basis of these analyses—in terms of deciding what to study—seems to develop later still, but here the research is too sparse for us to make conclusions with great confidence.

4

Knowledge and Memory Development

Let us begin with an unusual experiment by Chi (1978). Children (average age, 10 years) and adults were tested in two conditions. In one condition, they were to recall lists of ten digits; in the second, several stimuli were presented in an 8 × 8 array, and subjects were asked to reproduce the pattern on a blank array. Recall was tested immediately after presentation.

Thus far there is little about this experiment that would appear to warrant the description "unusual"; the study seems not unlike many of those discussed in previous chapters. The results, shown in Figure 4-1, are, however, quite different from any we have encountered before. For recall of digits, the familiar advantage of adults is seen. But for the arrays, children's recall exceeds adults' by more than 50 percent. This is a rare finding, one clearly deserving some attention.

Why should children's recall of arrays exceed that of adults by such a wide margin when exactly the opposite pattern is found for digits? There are some additional details of this experiment that shed light on this question. These were not ordinary arrays and

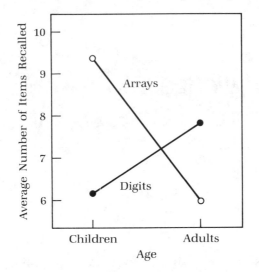

Figure 4-1 *Average number of digits and arrays recalled by children and adults. [Data from M. T. H. Chi, Knowledge structures and memory development. In R. Siegler (Ed.), Children's thinking: What develops? Hillsdale, N.J.: Lawrence Erlbaum Associates, Inc., 1978. Copyright 1978 by Lawrence Erlbaum Associates, Inc. Reprinted by permission.]*

stimuli, nor were these ordinary children. The arrays were chessboards, the stimuli were chess pieces, and the children were skilled chess players. The adults—research assistants and graduate students—lacked this detailed knowledge of chess. One other detail is important: The pieces were arranged on the board in positions taken from real chess games. For the skilled players, then, the positions were likely to be familiar *configurations;* for the adults, who were relatively ignorant of chess, they were random arrangements of pieces.

Usually, of course, older individuals are more likely to have the knowledge necessary to impute meaning to stimuli. For example, in a study by

Mandler and Robinson (1978), children from grades 1, 3, and 5 were shown eight complex pictures for ten seconds each. Half of the subjects at each grade saw pictures in which the objects were arranged in an organized, meaningful format. A window, chair, ladder, and trunk, for example, might be organized to depict a living room. The other half of the subjects saw exactly the same objects, but arranged in essentially an unorganized, random array. At all ages, recognition of organized pictures exceeded recognition of unorganized pictures, but the advantage for organized pictures was greater for older children. Somehow older children used the meaningful relationships in the organized pictures to improve their recognition, but the younger children did not.

How do these developmental advances in knowledge affect memory? Brown (1975, p. 116) drew on the work of Piaget and Inhelder (1973) and others to provide a succinct answer:

If memory and meaning depend on the subject's knowledge of the world. . . . The developmental implications are obvious; for there must be an intimate relationship between what the child can do or construct at a particular stage in his development and what he can remember or reconstruct. If the to-be-remembered material is meaningful and is congruent with the analyzing structures of the child, then comprehension of and subsequent memory for the essential features of that material will occur readily.

Thus, the match between information to be remembered and a child's cognitive structures—what Brown (1975) calls "head-fitting"—is critical for memory.

In this chapter, we will examine some of the many ways in which developmental changes in knowledge structures result in age differences in memory. We will begin with research by Piaget and Inhelder (1973) in which they studied how changes in knowledge are linked to changes in memory. Then we will turn to research that concerns the ways in which children's knowledge affects their retention of complex, meaningful "stimuli," such as paragraphs and stories. Finally, we consider the impact of sex-role stereotypes on memory.

Piagetian Research on Memory

Piaget's theory is our only comprehensive account of cognitive development, and thus it is not surprising that Piaget and his colleague Barbel Inhelder (Inhelder, 1969; Piaget and Inhelder, 1973) were the first to discuss the relation between knowledge and memory development. Their work has been reviewed in detail by Liben (1977a, 1977b); the description provided here is derived, in part, from these reviews.

Piaget and Inhelder (1973) focused on the way in which information stored in memory may change as the child develops. They believed that

The mnemonic code, far from being fixed and unchangeable, is structured and restructured along with general development. Such a restructuring of the code takes place in close dependence on the schemes of intelligence. The clearest indication of this is the observation of different types of memory organization in accordance with the age level of a child so that a *longer interval of retention without any new presentation, far from causing a deterioration of memory, may actually improve it.* (Inhelder, 1969, p. 361, emphasis added)

It is this latter prediction, that under some conditions memory might *improve* over time rather than decline, that makes Piaget and Inhelder's (1973) position so unusual and provocative. And, not surprisingly, this prediction has stimulated much research. Before considering this research, we need to examine the Piagetian view of memory change more carefully.

The best way to proceed is to consider an instance of cognitive developmental change and to show how Piaget and Inhelder (1973) relate this change to mnemonic functioning. A good choice would be children's understanding of an important component of quantitative thinking, namely, ordered relations. Numbers can be ordered easily. Given the digits 6, 24, 50, 12, 15, 49, an adult can easily order these numbers from largest to smallest or from smallest to largest, an operation called *seriation*. Adults can also order stimuli in the absence of obvious quantitative information. Examples would be ordering tones from highest to lowest, sandpaper from very fine to very coarse, and colors from very pale to very dark.

Piaget (1952) studied children's understanding of such ordered relations by giving the child a set of sticks of different lengths. The child was first asked to select the smallest stick. Then the child was asked to place the next larger stick adjacent to the first and to repeat this sequence until all sticks had been ordered correctly. Children in the middle preoperational period (roughly 4 to 5 years) were unable to order the sticks properly. By the late preoperational period (roughly 5 to 6 years), most children ordered the sticks, but only after considerable effort and frequent errors. With the emergence of concrete operations (around 7 years), children accomplished the task easily.

According to Piaget (see Flavell, 1963, chap. 5), these developmental changes in ordering reflect the growth of certain *grouping operations* during the early concrete operational period. With these operations as part of his mental apparatus, the child orders the sticks easily; without them, it is a hopeless task.

To examine links between memory development and cognitive development, Piaget and Inhelder (1973) examined 3- to 8-year-olds' retention of ordered arrays. Ten sticks, ordered from shortest to longest, were shown to children, who were told simply to study them in preparation for a memory test. A week later, they drew the sticks from memory. The drawings conformed to expectations based on Piaget's (1952) earlier work. Children in the 3- and 4-year-old group typically drew a set of lines of more or less equal length. The 4- and 5-year-olds produced an assortment of different types of drawings. Some drew several identical long and several identical short sticks. Others had three different sizes of otherwise identical sticks. Still other children drew seriated arrays but included only a few sticks. By 6 or 7 years, children drew the array correctly. In other words, each group drew the sticks in a way that corresponded to their level of understanding of seriation.

More startling are the longitudinal data from this experiment. Some six to eight months later, children were again asked to draw the array. Nearly 75 percent of the children drew pictures that were *more* accurate (i.e., more seriated) than their first attempts. Among the 5- to 8-year-olds, most of whom should be squarely in the transition from preoperational to concrete operational thought and thus acquiring the seriation scheme, 90 percent of the children drew pictures that were more seriated after the six-month interval.

What has happened in the intervening months? According to Inhelder (1969, p. 343),

During the interval . . . the [seriation] schemes themselves evolve because of their own inherent functioning through the spontaneous experiences and actions of the child. According to our hypothesis, the action schemes—in this particular case, the schemes of seriation—constitute the code for memorizing: this code is modified during the interval and the modified version is used as a new code. . . . At each stage, the memory image is symbolized according to the constraints of the corresponding code.

That is, children's knowledge of seriation increased over the six-month period, and their drawings reflected this increased knowledge by being more seriated (and hence more accurate) than they were originally. Stated in more familiar terms, the child's knowledge (i.e., his schemes) determines the way in which information is stored in and retrieved from memory.

Piaget and Inhelder's (1973) initial experiments have been replicated several times. The purpose of most of these investigations has been to devise more precise tests of Piaget and Inhelder's position. For example, Piaget and Inhelder do not predict that memory will always improve over a delay; memory improvement is expected only if the cognitive structures relevant to the memory stimuli have advanced. An experiment by Liben (1975b) with 5- and 9-year-olds is interesting in this light. She selected stimuli, shown in Figure 4-2, that tapped schemes that would be acquired at different developmental stages. The serial ordering concept (depicted in the first two pictures of Figure 4-2) should be transitional in 5-year-olds but well established in 9-year-olds; consequently, only the younger children's drawings should improve for these stimuli.

The concepts portrayed in the remaining four pictures are horizontality or verticality. As the names imply, *horizontality* refers to the child's understanding that the water level should be horizontal rather than parallel to the bottom of the bottle or bowl. The term *verticality* refers to the understanding that the wire on the crane and the flagpoles orient with reference to the true vertical rather than with reference to the surface of the hill. The latter concepts are more difficult than the seriation concept and typically are only transitional in 9-year-olds. Thus, no memory improvement would be expected for 5-year-olds, for whom the concepts are much too advanced. Some improvement would be expected for the transitional 9-year-olds.

Children drew all six pictures one week and again five months after the initial viewing. Children's drawings were grouped into three categories of accuracy. For example, on the ordered arrays, highly accurate drawings depicted the sticks in perfect seriated order; moderately accurate drawings contained portions that were seriated accurately; low-level drawings had no seriation. Drawings depicting the horizontality and verticality concepts were categorized in an analogous manner.

Children's drawings one week after the initial viewing were generally in accord with the predictions. On the seriation tasks, for example, nearly all 9-year-olds drew the nails in a perfectly seriated manner; 5-year-olds' drawings were more evenly distributed across the three categories (see Figure 4-3). A different configuration of results was found for the verticality tasks. When drawing the crane, for exam-

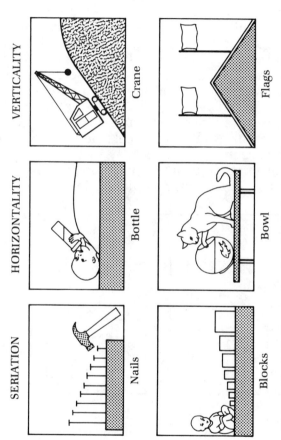

Figure 4-2 Pictures depicting concepts of seriation, horizontality, and verticality. [From L. S. Liben, Long-term memory for pictures related to seriation, horizontality, and verticality concepts. Developmental Psychology, 1975b, 11, 795–806. Copyright 1975 by the American Psychological Association. Reprinted by permission.]

ple, most 5-year-olds incorrectly drew the wire and ball at right angles to the side of the mountain. Many 9-year-olds' drawings were like this; however, the majority were more advanced, if not perfectly accurate (see Figure 4-3).

The longitudinal data are also generally consistent with Piaget and Inhelder's (1973) original work. Many children produced similar drawings on both occasions. For example, among 5-year-olds on the nails task—where long-term memory improvement would be expected—approximately half of the children produced drawings of the same level of accuracy after five months as after one week. However, when change did occur, it was generally in the expected direction of improvement. For example, the 5-year-olds' drawings of the seriated picture improved sig-

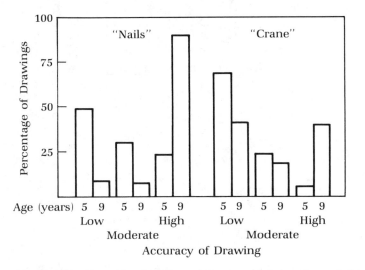

Figure 4-3 Percentage of 5- and 9-year-olds' drawings of the "nails" and "crane" pictures falling into three categories of accuracy. [Data from Liben (1975b).]

nificantly over the five-month span. The 9-year-olds' drawings of the four pictures concerning horizontality and verticality also improved significantly over the five-month span.

The general pattern of results from Liben's (1975b) study fits Piaget and Inhelder's (1973) position. If the knowledge associated with a particular memory stimulus develops during the retention interval, the child's drawings of the stimulus often reflect this newly acquired knowledge. In the absence of such knowledge, drawings do not change.

Another experiment by Liben (1975a) demonstrates a second way in which Piaget and Inhelder's (1973) prediction of long-term memory improvement has been examined. Liben's experiment used as a starting point the facts that (1) a child's cognitive structures and schemes develop "through the spontaneous experiences and actions of the child" (Inhelder, 1969, p. 343), and (2) this development results in changes in the memory code. A reasonable corollary to this view is that if we taught concepts such as horizontality and verticality to children—in effect simulating the changes that typically occur through the child's own activities—then these children should show greater memory improvement than should children who are not taught the concepts.

Liben (1975a) did exactly this with two groups of 8-year-olds. They were shown the crane stimulus depicted in Figure 4-2 and two weeks later were asked to draw the crane from memory. Approximately three months later, half of the children received extensive training on the concept of verticality. Finally, five months after they had viewed the crane initially, all children were asked to draw it again. Approximately 40 percent of the children who had learned about verticality drew "more vertical" drawings than they had at one week; only 14 percent of the untrained children did so. Furthermore, within the trained group, those children who had learned the most from the teaching tended to have the most improved drawings.

These experiments, as well as others (e.g., Maurer, Siegel, Lewis, Kristofferson, Barnes, and Levy, 1979), indicate that there is usually a significant correspondence between a child's comprehension of a stimulus and her immediate memory for that stimulus. The more controversial claim is that changes in memory occur in parallel with advances in a child's conceptual level. Here the evidence is not as compelling. Often a child's memory for a stimulus does not change over time (e.g., Liben, 1975a,b), and when such change occurs, it is not always linked to cognitive change (e.g., Maurer et al., 1979). These inconsistencies do not undermine Piaget and Inhelder's *general* claim that relevant knowledge can be an important component of mnemonic performance. However, knowledge is but one component of memory performance. Growth in the child's knowledge may lead to more accurate retention but, without development in the other domains of memory, may be insufficient to guarantee it.

Recall of Prose

Suppose we read the following paragraph to a subject:

The pitch came in over the plate. Everyone heard a loud "crack." In an instant, the ball sailed over the fence.

Later, if we asked the subject to recall the paragraph, we might hear something like this:

The pitcher threw the ball. The batter hit it hard. It was a home run.

Several discrepancies exist between what was heard originally and what was recalled. The most interesting of these center on the words *pitcher, batter,* and *home run.* None of these words was presented originally. Each was inferred from the context. That is, the subject deduced that the paragraph concerned baseball and then made several inferences based on his knowledge of the game. Thus, from "The ball sailed over the fence," he inferred that the batter hit a home run.

What we see in this example is the *constructive* aspect of memory. People use their knowledge to embellish, elaborate, and otherwise "go beyond the information given" as they represent information in memory. A consequence of this tendency is that verbatim recall of complicated, meaningful stimuli is often quite poor but rarely is the meaning or gist of a passage lost (Bartlett, 1932).

One important function of knowledge is to allow a person to "fill gaps" that may exist in information that is to be remembered. Thus, in the example paragraph about baseball, the hypothetical subject could use knowledge about baseball to derive certain conclusions about the paragraph. In like manner, if a child is asked to remember the sentence "The workman dug a hole in the ground," she may use her knowledge to infer spontaneously the presence of a shovel. In fact, studies by Paris and his colleagues (Paris and Lindauer, 1976; Paris, Lindauer, and Cox,

1977) have shown that the tendency to make inferences such as this develops considerably during the elementary school years. Subjects in the first study (Paris and Lindauer, 1976) were read sentences such as the following: (1) "His mother baked a cake *in the oven*" and (2) "Her friend swept the kitchen floor *with a broom.*" Each sentence described an action performed by an individual. Half the sentences included the instrument usually used to perform the activity (i.e., the italicized portion of the example sentences); in the other half, the instruments were deleted. Later, the instruments were provided as cues to help remember the sentences. The experimenter might have said, for example, "What sentence does *broom* remind you of?" Paris and Lindauer (1976) argued that if children spontaneously infer the presence of the instrument, then that instrument should be an equally effective retrieval cue regardless of whether it was actually presented or not.

The results are shown in Figure 4-4. Instrument cues were useful to 11-year-olds both when the instruments had actually been presented and when they had to be inferred. For 7- and 9-year-olds, however, the instrument cues were much less effective when the instrument had not been presented originally. Apparently only the oldest children routinely inferred the presence of the instruments as the sentences were presented and incorporated these instruments into their mnemonic representations of the sentences.

Much the same pattern of developmental change was found by Paris, Lindauer, and Cox (1977). This study differed from its predecessor only in that the inferences concerned the *consequences* of actions rather than the instruments used to perform the actions. For example: "He accidentally played in

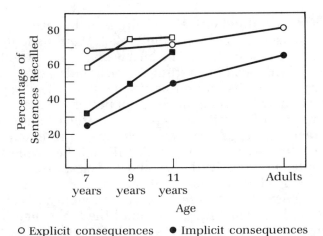

○ Explicit consequences   ● Implicit consequences
□ Explicit instruments   ■ Implicit instruments

Figure 4-4 *Percentage of sentences recalled as a function of age and type of cue. [Data from Paris and Lindauer (1976) and Paris, Lindauer, and Cox (1977).]*

poison ivy *and itched.*" As before, the consequences were sometimes stated explicitly and sometimes had to be inferred. When the consequences were given as retrieval cues, only adults used them effectively regardless of whether they had been presented or not (see Figure 4-4). At the other extreme, consequences were of little help to 7-year-olds unless they had been stated explicitly. Combining the data of the two studies, it seems that by age 11 children will infer the instrument of an action but they may not routinely infer the consequences of an action until they are several years older.

Thus far we have considered inferences that are derived from a single word or sentence. Another important form of inference involves integrating the information from several sentences to arrive at a new piece of information. For example, suppose a child read the following: (1) "The bird is in the cage" and (2) "The cage is on top of the table." Would she spontaneously infer that "The bird is on top of the table"?

Evidence from a study by Paris and Carter (1973) suggests that children as young as age 7 *do* spontaneously integrate information in this manner. Children heard a series of "stories" like the example just given. Later, several sentences were presented and children were asked to judge if each had been presented previously. Both 7- and 10-year-olds frequently judged that inferential statements had actually been presented before. That is, they were quite confident that "The bird is on top of the table" had been presented, when in fact it had not been presented. And these errors in false recognition of inferences were not caused by generally poor performance: With the exception of the inferential statements, children made few errors. For example, children rarely "recognized" inferences that were semantically inconsistent with what they had heard (e.g., "The bird is under the table").

However, Liben and Posnansky (1977) suggested that children may not have made inferences, even though they falsely recognized inferential sentences. They pointed out that the inferential statements contained the same nouns and relational terms as the original sentences. Furthermore, the words in the inferential sentences occurred in the same positions as they had in the original sentences. Perhaps children were recognizing the inferential sentences because the words and their positions seemed familiar, rather than because they had integrated the sentences.

Liben and Posnansky (1977) evaluated this possibility by conducting a variation of the Paris and Carter (1973) study. The sole difference was that their recognition test included inferential sentences in which the word order and relational terms had been changed. Thus, in the examples given earlier, the additional inferential sentence would have been "The table is under the bird." This sentence differs from the original sentence in that *table* is now the first word in the sentence rather than the last, *bird* is now last rather than the first, and the relational term is *under* rather than *on top of.* Liben and Posnansky found that 8-year-olds reliably "recognized" inferences even when the word order and relational terms had been changed but that 5- and 6-year-olds did not. Only the older children integrated the original sentences to derive a memory representation that included relationships among all objects in the story. Younger children were apparently more likely to remember the sentences individually. (Small and Butterworth, 1981, reach a similar conclusion with different procedures.)

From what we have seen thus far, it would be easy to conclude that integration is restricted to verbal material. However, quite the contrary is true. Integration is readily demonstrated whenever there is meaning to be abstracted from separate elements and linked in a unified representation. Pezdek (1980; Pezdek and Miceli, 1982; see also Paris and Mahoney, 1974; Duncan, Whitney, and Kunen, 1982) has shown that information acquired in one mode (e.g., via pictures) is readily integrated with information acquired in a different mode (e.g., via sentences). In Pezdek's first study, subjects first saw 24 stimuli consisting of 12 pictures and 12 sentences, arranged randomly. Following these 24 stimuli were 24 additional stimuli, each corresponding to one of the original 24 stimuli. As can be seen in Figure 4-5, if the stimulus in the first set of 24 was a picture, its counterpart in the second set was a sentence (and vice-versa). Half the corresponding pairs were unrelated to one another; in the other half, the second stimulus was consistent with the original stimulus but added a new detail. Thus, in the example at the top of Figure 4-5, the first stimulus was simply "The girl enjoyed playing the sport"; the added detail in the corresponding picture is that the sport is tennis. In the example at the bottom of Figure 4-5, the first stimulus is a picture of a woman's hand with several rings; the corresponding sentence adds *bracelet:* "The woman wearing the bracelet wore several rings."

During the test phase, the original 24 stimuli were shown, along with 24 stimuli describing the information in the intervening items *but in the mode of the original stimuli,* as shown in Figure 4-5. The key issue was whether, on a recognition test, subjects would claim that they had seen the stimuli actually presented, or whether they would "recognize" the stimulus that integrated the original information and the additional detail provided by the second set of 24 stimuli.

The sixth-graders and high school students did misrecognize stimuli in the test phase; that is, they apparently spontaneously added the new information provided by the second set of 24 stimuli to the information derived from the first set of 24. The third-graders did not integrate information in this way; however, in a subsequent experiment in which a slower rate of presentation was used—thereby allowing more time for these integrative processes to occur—third-graders did integrate information in exactly the same manner as did sixth-graders and high school students (Pezdek and Miceli, 1982).

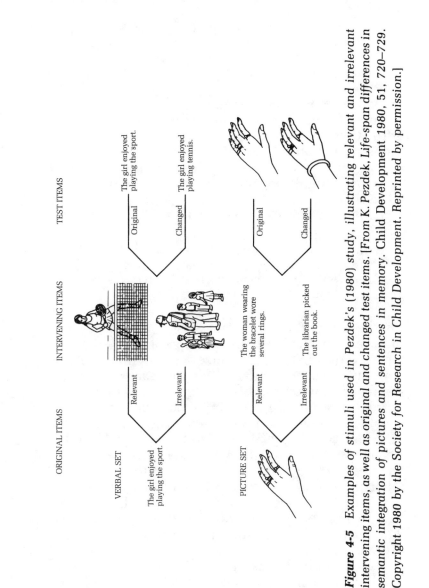

Figure 4-5 Examples of stimuli used in Pezdek's (1980) study, illustrating relevant and irrelevant intervening items, as well as original and changed test items. [From K. Pezdek, Life-span differences in semantic integration of pictures and sentences in memory. Child Development 1980, 51, 720–729. Copyright 1980 by the Society for Research in Child Development. Reprinted by permission.]

Thus, integration is not specific to any particular mode of presentation. Regardless of the mode in which information is presented, by age 8, children are prone to construct holistic representations of information that represent the important semantic relations contained in that information.

In the work described thus far, the inferences have been highly specific, focusing on interpretation of individual words or sentences. More global inferences also occur. Consider the following paragraph:

The little boy paid the money to the woman. He took the ticket from her and gave it to the man standing at the door. Then he went inside to look for a seat. Soon it was dark and the _____ began.

By the end of the paragraph, most readers will have inferred that the boy is in a theater, or perhaps a ball park. Notice that this inference does not hinge on any particular word or sentence. Instead, each successive sentence provides additional clues that allow us to formulate a more precise inference about the boy's acts. The paragraph's first sentence can be interpreted in a number of ways. However, learning early in the second sentence that the boy received a ticket for his money, we know that this constrains the number of plausible situations, for young children buy tickets only at amusement parks, swimming pools, theaters, and ball parks. In succeeding sentences, we use our knowledge to constrain even further our interpretation of this paragraph.

Elaboration of passages in this manner has been studied by a number of investigators. A study by Brown, Smiley, Day, Townsend, and Lawton (1977) is instructive (see also Harris, Mandias, Terwogt, and

Tjintjelaar, 1980). Children in grades 2 through 7 heard a brief story about a young man of the fictitious Targa people. Some children had been told previously that the Targa were Eskimos; others had been led to believe that the Targa were desert Indians. After listening to the story twice, children were asked to recall it in their own words.

One way to assess the impact of the subjects' knowledge of the Targa on their recall of the passage is in terms of the frequency with which they "recall" information that was not actually presented. For example, the passage included the phrase "The weather was bad. . . ." Children who had been told that the Targa were Eskimos were likely to recall this phrase in words such as, "It was cold and icy . . ."; subjects who understood the Targa to be desert Indians recalled it, instead, as "It was hot and dry. . . ." Intrusion of such knowledge of the Targa during recall occurred at all ages but increased from 51 percent among second-graders to 79 percent among seventh-graders. It is evident in these results that even young children often do not distinguish between what was presented from what they know about what was presented. To the contrary, children elaborate a story with whatever knowledge they can bring to bear and do so more often as they grow older. As Brown et al. (1977, p. 1464) describe it: "The intrusions were creative errors as they added to the cohesion and coherence of the story that was remembered and probably helped initially in rendering the material interpretable."

Inferences of this sort are not always helpful. They can interfere with performance when the aim is verbatim recall. A study by Landis (1982) illustrates this phenomenon. Passages were read aloud to 7- and 10-year-olds. For some children, the passage dealt with a well-known historical figure (e.g., Abraham Lincoln). For other children, the same passage was used with the name of the historical figure replaced by a fictitious person (e.g., Robert Baker). During a subsequent recognition memory test, individual sentences were presented, including (1) some sentences from the passage (e.g., Abe/Robert decided that, if he ever got the chance, he would fight slavery), (2) sentences that dealt with known facts about the historical figure but that had not been presented (e.g., Abraham Lincoln/Robert Baker was born in a log cabin), and (3) some sentences unrelated to the topic of the passage (e.g., Abe's/Robert's first relative to come to this country was a weaver). The key finding is that children who heard the passage about the historical figure had great difficulty distinguishing between those sentences they had actually heard about the person from those not presented that dealt with known facts about the historical figure. This confusion was *not* a byproduct of generally poor recognition, for children were quite accurate in judging that sentences in the final category had not been presented. In contrast, children who heard the sentences as part of a paragraph about a fictitious person had little difficulty identifying only those sentences they actually had heard.

Another byproduct of these constructive processes is that memory is sometimes *distorted* in the direction of one's knowledge. Suppose children are told stories about familiar people in which those people are depicted in an unorthodox fashion: The *Six Million Dollar Man* is described as weak, and the *Bionic Woman* is referred to as ugly. Over time, children remember characters in these stories as being strong and beautiful—their usual attributes—rather than as they were described in the story (Ceci, Caves, and Howe, 1981).

Sex-Role Stereotypes and Memory

By the time children enter elementary school, they have extensive knowledge of sex-typed activities and interests. They believe that girls play with dolls and like to sew; boys prefer to build things and play sports. These stereotypes of masculine and feminine behavior—like any other form of knowledge—can exert a great deal of influence on the way experiences are perceived and remembered.

Consider first the findings of a study by Kail and Levine (1976). In this experiment, there were five recall trials, each consisting of (1) presentation of two words to be remembered; (2) a distracting task, naming colors, for 15 seconds; and (3) an interval during which the child attempted to recall *only* the two words presented on that trial. For trials 1 to 4 some children were presented words that connoted masculine games and objects (e.g., hunting, airplane); other children were presented words that connoted feminine games and objects (e.g., hopscotch, dolls). Notice, in Figure 4-6, that recall steadily declined on each successive trial. This reflects *proactive interference*—the interfering effects of previous, similar material on recall. On the fifth trial, which followed the previous four without interruption, children in a control group were asked to recall two additional words with the same sex-role connotations as those presented on trials 1 to 4. For children in the experimental group, the connotations of words were changed: Those children who had been presented words with masculine connotations now heard words with feminine connotations, and vice-versa. As can be seen in Figure 4-6, recall by children in the experimental group increased significantly on trial 5, but recall by children in the control group did not.

Recall improved in the experimental group because the words with the novel sex-role connotations were not subject to proactive interference. Furthermore, this increase in recall does not depend upon the "conscious" recognition of the novel sex-role connotations, for children typically could not describe how words on trial 5 differed from those presented on previous trials. In other words, it appears as if children's knowledge of sex-typed behaviors allows them

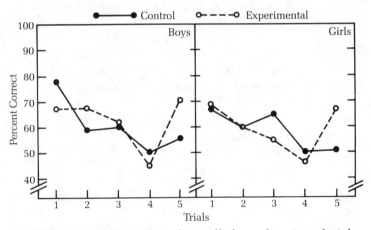

Figure 4-6 *Percentage of words recalled as a function of trials for children in the experimental and control conditions. [Data from Kail and Levine (1976).]*

to store or *encode* these words in memory differently, so that they are not subject to interference from words presented previously.

Knowledge of sex-typed behavior, like all forms of knowledge, can bias interpretation and recall of our experiences. For example, when children are asked to remember the actions of boys and girls behaving in nonstereotypic fashion, it is often the case in recall that children will transform the sex of the actor to make it consistent with sex-role knowledge. Shown a picture of a girl sawing wood, 5-year-olds are likely to remember it as a picture of a boy, not a girl (Martin and Halversòn, 1983). Similarly, told a story about a boy who picks flowers, 10-year-olds often remember that the flowers were picked by a girl (Koblinsky, Cruse, and Sugawara, 1978).

Memory distortions like these can be avoided if children are forewarned that stereotypic knowledge may not be appropriate for a particular boy or girl. Koblinsky and Cruse (1981) created stories in which a boy and a girl each displayed four stereotypically masculine behaviors and four stereotypically feminine behaviors. Thus, each story included eight behaviors that were consistent with sex-role stereotypes and eight that were not. Later, each of the 16 behaviors from the story was presented, and 10-year-olds were asked to recall if it had been the boy or girl who behaved in a particular way. Here children's retention was much more accurate for sex-role consistent behaviors (90 percent) than for sex-role inconsistent behaviors (60 percent). A different pattern occurred when the stories were preceded by a description of the boy or girl suggesting that traditional stereotypes might be inappropriate. For example, some children were told:

This is a story about a girl named Mary and a boy named Bill. Mary is different from most girls. Her best friends are boys and she would rather play with boys than girls. When Mary grows up, she wants to become a pilot.

When children were given information of this type, the usual memory bias was eliminated completely. In fact, alerted that the child in the story was not typical, subjects' retention of sex-role inconsistent behaviors was actually somewhat larger than their retention of sex-role consistent behaviors (82 percent versus 72 percent).

Research on sex-role stereotypes and memory makes it clear that knowledge can be both a mnemonic asset and a mnemonic liability. On the positive side, inferences based on knowledge allow children to create more elaborate, meaningful representations in memory of their experiences. Yet, this occurs at the cost of introducing distortion into their recall of those experiences. Children often experience difficulty distinguishing what they actually saw, heard, or felt in a situation from what they *usually* see, hear, or feel in that situation.

Summary

As children grow older, they acquire more knowledge about their world, and this acquisition has profound effects on their efforts to remember. In the first part of this chapter, we examined Piaget and Inhelder's (1973) work on memory change. Several studies examined the effects of acquiring new conceptual schemes on the representation of information that had originally been stored in memory with less advanced schemes. Specifically, the acquisition of three schemes—seriation, verticality, and horizontality—was shown to influence memory for stimuli related to these schemes. In addition, the unusual finding here was that such representations sometimes became more accurate over time instead of deteriorating.

In the second part of this chapter, the focus was on the role of knowledge in memory for prose. Here an important developmental acquisition is the ability to make inferences, for this allows a child to integrate information to be remembered. Furthermore, through inferential skills and his own prior knowledge, a child can elaborate and embellish information to be remembered. We saw that 11-year-olds typically infer the instruments associated with an activity, but not until adulthood do people consistently infer the consequences usually associated with an action. By age 8, children spontaneously integrate the material in simple paragraphs into a single, coherent, mnemonic representation.

Finally, it was shown that a person's knowledge can bias the way experiences are remembered, distorting them in the direction of typical experiences. These distortions were illustrated, in the third part of the chapter, with the special case of the impact of sex-role knowledge on memory.

A final comment is necessary concerning the research discussed here. In some respects, the topics discussed in this chapter are more diverse than those of previous chapters. This diversity of topics under the single heading of "Knowledge and Memory Development" should alert us to the fact that there is no single relation between the two. Conceptual development encompasses a number of different forms of intellectual growth, each of which may be linked to memory in its own unique way. It is safe to say that, in looking at inference making, the schemes of seriation, horizontality, and verticality, and the impact of sex-role stereotyping, we have barely begun to examine these relations. Specifying these links and tracing their development remain major goals for future theories of memory development.

5

Early Memory

During the first 6 months of life the infant is considered to be especially vulnerable to the evil eye as well as illness and is carefully cared for by the mother. The infant is fed on demand at the slightest indication of hunger or distress. He is rarely taken from the dark interior of his home. During the day he is swaddled and sleeps in a hanging cradle with his face usually covered. . . . During the first 6 months, the mother generally is the exclusive caretaker; brothers and sisters are not allowed to hold or play with the young child. Variety of sensory experience is reduced to a minimum. The infant sees relatively few people and experiences little direct social interaction. (Kagan, Klein, Finley, Rogoff, and Nolan, 1979, pp. 9–10)

These practices, which exist in villages on the shores of Lake Atitlán in the highlands of Guatemala, no doubt strike many readers as frightful. At the very least, they certainly contrast with experiences typical for babies of middle-class parents in industrialized societies, where infants are often stimulated from birth with conversation, "educational toys," and the like.

Our surprise at the rearing conditions in Guatemala arises, in part, because of our beliefs about the impact of early experience on human development. Beginning with Plato, and continuing through Rousseau and Freud, scholars have often claimed that experiences early in life are special, having a greater impact on development than those occurring later in life (Wachs and Gruen, 1982). What may not be obvious is that our beliefs in early experience presuppose a theory about memory in very young children. We have "conversations" with a 2-month-old, in part because we assume those conversations will influence subsequent linguistic and social skills. Of course, the "conversations" can influence later skills only if the infant remembers them, in some form. That is, future behavior can be influenced by current experiences only if those experiences are stored in memory.

These early memory skills are the focus of this chapter. We first discuss research that concerns the emergence of memory skills in the first year of life. Then we discuss *infantile amnesia*, which refers to the inability of adults to remember events from early in their lives.

Growth of Memory in Infancy

Recognition in Newborns

In light of the many age-related changes in memory that we have seen thus far, it is quite natural to ask "When does memory 'begin'?" That is, what is the youngest age at which humans can remember previous experiences? However, we immediately run into an obstacle in an effort to answer these questions: Most of the methods that are used to study memory in children and adults require the subject to verbalize his response, and thus they are quite inappropriate for infants. What is needed is some response that is well mastered by the infant. Looking is such a behavior. For example, only a few minutes after birth neonates will look in the direction of a sound (Wertheimer, 1961). Furthermore, just a few weeks after birth infants will track a stimulus as it moves in front of them (Bower, Broughton, and Moore, 1971).

Having found a suitable response for infants, we next need to create a task in which we can use this response to make inferences about what infants remember. The most commonly used procedure—called the *habituation* paradigm—involves showing a series of patterns to an infant and measuring how long the infant looks at the pattern. Figure 5-1 shows how a laboratory might be set up to do this. Slides are projected onto a screen placed directly in front of the infant. An observer, seated behind the screen, watches the infant's eyes through holes near the edge of the screen. Because the cornea of the infant's eye reflects the focus of the infant's gaze, the observer can record precisely how much time the infant spends looking at the pattern.

One way to use this procedure to study memory would be to let an infant look at a pattern for as long as she wants. Then after a delay, we show her two patterns: one the pattern just seen; the second, a new pattern. If she looks primarily at the new pattern, this probably indicates that the infant is distinguishing between the novel and the familiar stimuli.

Of course, infants might look at one pattern rather than another for several reasons that are unre-

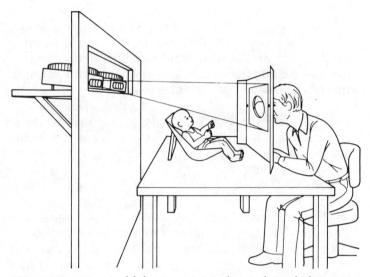

Figure 5-1 A typical laboratory setup for studying habituation in infants. Stimuli are projected onto a screen in front of the infant. An observer monitors the infant's gaze through the holes near the edge of the screen. [From G. M. Olson and T. Sherman, Attention, learning, and memory in infants. In M. M. Haith and J. Campos (Eds.), Handbook of child psychology, Vol. 2. New York: Wiley, 1983. Copyright 1983 by John Wiley and Sons. Redrawn with permission.]

lated to memory. Infants may find some patterns more interesting to look at than others. For example, 3- to 5-month-olds seem to prefer a bull's-eye to a series of stripes (Fantz, Fagan, and Miranda, 1975). To control for infant preferences, all stimuli in an experiment are used both as novel and familiar stimuli. In other words, infants would be divided into two groups. The memory test for both groups would involve a bull's-eye paired with a set of stripes. One group would see the bull's-eye prior to seeing both stimuli; the other group would see the stripes. If both groups looked longer at the new pattern (stripes for the first group, bull's-eye for the second), we have evidence for infant memory.

Friedman and his associates (Friedman, 1972a, 1972b; Friedman, Bruno, and Vietze, 1974; see also work by Slater, Morison, and Rose, 1982) have conducted a series of studies using procedures such as these to demonstrate that newborns recognize familiar stimuli. In one study (Friedman, 1972a), 1- to 4-day-olds were shown a black and white checkerboard. For some infants, the checkerboard included four squares; other infants saw a checkerboard with 144 squares. The checkerboards were shown for 60 seconds, during which time an observer recorded the amount of time the infant looked at the checkerboard.

Initially, infants looked at the checkerboard for most of the 60 seconds. After the checkerboard had been presented several additional times, infants looked for only 45 seconds, a significant decline. One explanation for this difference, of course, is that the infants recognized the checkerboard from previous trials and were less "interested" in it, so they looked less. A second possibility—quite plausible with newborns—is that the infants were simply tired and less prone to look at any object, familiar or novel. To distinguish between these possibilities, Friedman (1972a) divided the infants into two groups. Some saw the checkerboard again; others saw a novel checkerboard—the 144-square checkerboard if they had previously seen the 4-square board, and vice-versa. If the decline in looking over trials reflected general fatigue, infants should not look any longer at the novel stimulus than at the familiar one; if the decline reflects disinterest in an ever more familiar checkerboard, then looking should increase for the novel board. In fact, looking at the novel board increased to approximately 50 to 55 seconds, consistent with the interpretation that infants recognized the familiar checkerboard.

The work of Friedman and his colleagues demonstrates that newborns are capable of visual recognition of stimuli that they have just seen repeatedly. Work by DeCasper and Fifer (1980) broadens these conclusions. In this study, newborns sucked on a nipple that was linked to tape recorders in such a way that sucking caused a tape to play. The nipple was first placed in the infant's mouth for seven minutes during which sucking did not activate the tape. Then the procedure was changed so that if the infant sucked more rapidly than before, a tape of the mother's voice played continuously; if the infant sucked less rapidly, a tape of an unfamiliar woman's voice played continuously. Most infants changed their rate of sucking in order to hear their mother's voice instead of the stranger's. Furthermore, when the contingency was changed again, so that slower sucking produced the mother's voice, the newborns changed their sucking once again. Infants apparently recognized their mother's voice and sucked to gain repeated presentation of the voice. This is particularly interesting because the infants had had no more than 12 hours of contact with their mothers since birth.

Collectively, the work of Friedman (e.g., 1972a, 1972b) and DeCasper and Fifer (1980) indicates that newborns recognize events they have seen or heard previously. We know little of how newborns remember experiences from other senses. Breast-feeding, for example, is a visual-auditory-olfactory-gustatory-thermotactile experience for both mother and infant. Which of these aspects of feeding represents the newborn's memory for the experience? Extrapolating from work with other newborn mammals (e.g.,

Alberts, 1984; Gottlieb, 1971), human newborns may well remember the thermotactile and gustatory aspects of nursing (e.g., the warmth and feel of the mother's breast, the warmth, texture, and taste of her milk), rather than the auditory or visual characteristics. Studies of newborns' memories for these experiences would certainly provide a broader picture of human memory at birth and might indicate greater mnemonic competence in newborns, as the auditory and visual systems are less well developed at birth than are some other sensory systems (e.g., Alberts, 1984; Aslin, 1984).

The First Six Months

Research on memory in older infants has much the same flavor as work with newborns. Among the most extensive work on memory in older infants is that of Fagan (1970, 1973), who has shown that infants' recognition memory is surprisingly durable. This is seen clearly in two experiments (Fagan, 1973, Experiments 1 and 2). In the first experiment, squares arranged in checkerboard patterns were shown to infants for two minutes. Either immediately, or after delays of 24 or 48 hours, this pattern was paired with novel patterns and shown for a total of 20 seconds. Infants looked consistently longer at the novel stimuli, regardless of the length of time between initial viewing of the stimulus and the "memory test." Infants clearly are capable of recognizing complicated patterns after a two-day period.

More impressive, because of the length of the delay involved, are the results of a second experiment by Fagan (1973, Experiment 2). The procedures of the previous experiment were modified in two ways.

First, the stimuli were black-and-white photographs of human faces rather than patterns. Second, recognition was measured after five intervals: 3, 24, and 48 hours and one and two weeks. The subjects were 6-month-olds. The results are easily summarized. At all retention intervals, infants looked reliably longer at the novel stimuli. The important implication of these results is, as Fagan (1973, p. 448) describes it, "that long-term recognition memory for pictorial stimuli is a very basic ability occurring . . . in the early months of life."

The infants in Fagan's (1970, 1973) research were approximately 6 months old. An obvious question is whether long-term recognition memory would be as accurate in younger infants or whether it would be detected at all. There is little relevant evidence; most of the research has been done with infants who are at least 4 months old. An experiment by Martin (1975), however, provides some insights into recognition memory in younger infants. Three groups of infants, 2-, 3½-, and 5-month olds, were tested on two successive days. On the first day, a geometric figure was shown for 30 seconds, six times. A day later, the figure was shown an additional six times, again for 30 seconds each. If infants recognized the figure on the second day, they should have looked at it less than they did originally. The results are shown in Figure 5.2. The predicted pattern was found for all groups of infants: At all ages, infants looked less at the stimuli on the second day. Moreover, the difference in looking increased slightly with age. The 5-month-olds, in particular, looked very little at the stimuli on the second day. Although the greater decline for older infants was not statistically significant, it does suggest that recognition memory is maturing between the ages of 2 and 5 months. That is, 2-month-old infants

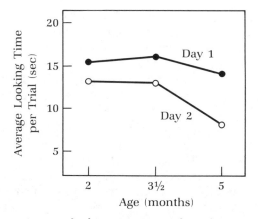

Figure 5-2 *Average looking time per trial as a function of age for days 1 and 2. [Data from Martin (1975).]*

are capable of recognition after a period of 24 hours, but apparently not with the same precision of older infants.

The studies by Martin (1975) and Fagan (1970, 1973) are representative of a very large literature in which many aspects of visual recognition memory have been examined in 2- to 6-month-olds. Common to almost all these studies is that memory is assessed via some version of the habituation procedure. As a general rule, such a single-minded approach to a phenomenon is never sound; conclusions are invariably broader and can be drawn with greater confidence when they are based on findings from a number of paradigms. Furthermore, the habituation procedure has been criticized on a number of specific grounds. One problem, noted by Sophian (1980), is that inferences about memory require that infants both remember the familiar stimulus and look systematically longer at a novel stimulus. When such preferential looking does not occur, this may be due to infants' forgetting the familiar stimulus; another possibility, though, is that infants do remember the familiar stimulus but find both the novel and familiar patterns equally attractive.

A related problem occurs when making age comparisons. Recall that in Martin's (1975) study, older infants looked less at the familiar stimuli than did younger infants. I interpreted this as an indication of greater retention by older infants; it might simply mean, however, that preference for novelty is not as strong in younger babies (see Carter and Strauss, 1981, and Sophian, 1980, 1981, for a full discussion of these issues).

Another criticism of the habituation procedure concerns the nature of the memory skills that are measured. As Rovee-Collier and Fagen (1981) noted, with the habituation paradigm, analysis

. . . terminates with response to [the novel stimulus]; it provides no mechanism by which to measure whether the infant can use the information recognized in [the familiar stimulus]. When carried to a logical conclusion, this model describes the processing and storage of stimulus attributes to which an infant will systematically not attend in the future. It is difficult to conceptualize the evolutionary advantage of such a memory system. (p. 226)

The cumulative impact of this and other criticisms is an awareness that the habituation paradigm should be supplemented with other procedures (Sophian, 1980). Rovee-Collier and her colleagues (e.g., 1984; Fagen & Rovee-Collier, 1982; Rovee-Collier & Fagen, 1981), in particular, have used a conjugate reinforcement procedure to study memory in 2- to 4-month-olds. A mobile is placed above an infant's crib, as shown in Figure 5-3. A ribbon connects the mobile to

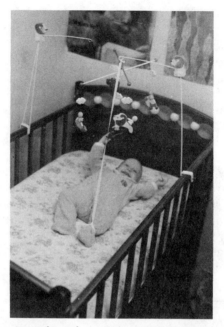

Figure 5-3 *An infant during the reinforcement phase of the conjugate reinforcement paradigm. The mobile is connected to the infant's ankle by the ribbon and moves in direct proportion to the frequency and vigor of the infant's kicks. (Photograph courtesy of Carolyn Rovee-Collier.)*

one of the infant's ankles so that kicking moves the mobile. When the ribbon is not connected to the mobile, an alert 3-month-old will kick between five and ten times a minute. When the ribbon is attached to the infant's ankle, kicking doubles in frequency, indicating that babies have learned the relation between their actions and the movement of the mobile.

To measure memory, the procedure is repeated later. If an infant remembers perfectly the impact of kicking on the mobile, then kicking should be just as frequent at the beginning of a subsequent session as it was at the *end* of the first session (when infants had doubled their kicking). If an infant has forgotten the relation between kicking and the action of the mobile, then kicking should revert to the frequency seen at the *beginning* of the first session, when the ribbon was not attached to the ankle.

The data in Figure 5-4, from a study by Rovee-Collier, Sullivan, Enright, Lucas, and Fagen (1980) show how well 3-month-olds remember the contingency between kicking and the motion of the mobile. In this figure, a retention ratio of 1.0 indicates perfect retention; scores of .3 to .4 indicate total forgetting. Hence, infants appear to remember this contingency reliably for a week, a much longer interval than had been thought possible based on work with habituation procedures (e.g., Werner and Perlmutter, 1979).

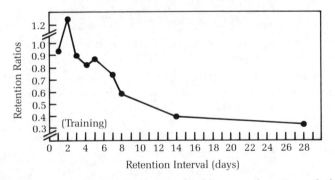

Figure 5-4 *Retention by 3-month-olds as a function of the amount of time elapsed since they learned the contingency. A retention ratio of 1.0 indicates perfect retention; scores of approximately .3 to .4 indicate complete forgetting. [From C. K. Rovee-Collier, M. W. Sullivan, M. Enright, D. Lucas, and J. Fagen, Reactivation of infant memory. Science, 1980, 208, 1159–1161. Copyright 1980 by the American Association for the Advancement of Science. Reprinted by permission.]*

Younger babies learn the contingency between kicking and the mobile's movement as rapidly as older ones, but they differ in retention: 3-month-olds remember the contingency for 8, but not 14, days, and 2-month-olds do so for 3, but not 6, days (Vander Linde, cited in Rovee-Collier, 1984).

The habituation and reinforcement procedures differ in their estimates of how long infants can remember information, but both support the conclusion that memory improves in the first few months of life.

What is responsible for these age differences in retention? One possibility is that, although all infants retain enough information to recognize a pattern as familiar soon after it is presented, older infants remember more of this information and thus can recognize a pattern after a longer interval. As an example, let us imagine that two infants are shown a large gold star several times. A day later, we repeat this procedure. If one infant remembers that she has seen a large gold star, she will probably look at the star only briefly on the second day. In contrast, if the second infant remembers that he has seen a large star, but has forgotten the color, he probably will look longer than the first infant, but less than a third infant would who had never seen the star previously.

There is no evidence to support this suggestion directly. However, it is at least plausible, for Strauss and Cohen (1980) have shown that 5-month-olds forget aspects of a stimulus at different rates. Procedures like those devised by Fagan (1970, 1973) were used. Infants viewed a simple form (either an arrow or a "Y") for 60 seconds. A memory test followed immediately or after delays of either 15 minutes or 24 hours. In the memory test, the familiar stimulus was paired with a stimulus that was identical in three aspects but different in one. For example, an infant might first see a large, black *upright* arrow, which is later paired with a large, black *rotated* arrow. The stimuli in this case would be alike in size, color, and form but different in orientation. If the infant pays equal attention to the two stimuli, then information about the orientation of the original stimulus apparently has been forgotten. By varying the dimensions that were similar and different, Strauss and Cohen (1980) hoped to discover how long infants remembered different aspects of stimuli. They found that immediately after presentation, infants retained information about all four aspects of stimuli; 15 minutes later, they remembered only information about form and color, and 24 hours later, they remembered only the form of the stimulus. Thus, this study provides evidence that various types of information may be lost from infant memory at different rates. The missing link, of course, is to show that some types of information are lost more rapidly by younger infants than by older ones.

Thus far I have suggested that younger infants forget more readily because they store less information about the stimulus. Another possibility is that younger infants are less skilled at retrieving information they have stored. The most convincing evidence for this point of view is based on a phenomenon known as *reinstatement*, which was first demonstrated by Campbell and Jaynes (1966). Reinstatement refers to a brief reencounter with some part of an experience that results in retention in circumstances in which forgetting would occur ordinarily. Furthermore, this reencounter is so brief that no additional learning takes place; instead, the reencounter seems to "remind" the organism of the original learning.

A study by Sullivan (1982) illustrates the reinstatement phenomenon. Some 3-month-olds were tested using Rovee-Collier's conjugate reinforcement procedures. These infants remembered the contingency between kicking and the mobile's movement quite well one day after learning but apparently had forgotten it 14 days later. The same procedures were also used with a second group of 3-month-olds, with one twist: 13 days after training, these babies were reminded of their training experience. With the babies sitting upright, the mobile was placed over their cribs as before, but *the experimenter pulled the ribbon* at approximately the same rate at which the infant had kicked in the previous session. When these infants' retention was tested the next day—now 14 days since their original learning—their recall of the contingency was quite accurate. The ribbon was not attached to the infant's ankle during the reminder experience; hence, the infants' improved retention cannot reflect additional learning during this time. Instead, reinstatement somehow aids retrieval of information that is still available in memory but that otherwise would be inaccessible.

Similar reinstatement effects have been observed with younger (Davis and Rovee-Collier, 1983) and older infants (Cornell, 1979). Apparently, younger infants may often be unable to demonstrate retention because they fail to retrieve stored experiences. What remains to be shown is that younger infants are more susceptible than older ones to retrieval failure, and that this greater susceptibility is a key determinant of their poorer retention.

This is but one of many gaps in our knowledge of infants' recognition memory skills. However, we should not let our ignorance of the details of infant memory obscure a very important finding that emerges consistently in these studies: The young infant is an unexpectedly capable memorizer. (For thor ough reviews of research on infant memory, see Cohen and Gelber, 1975; Olson and Sherman, 1983; Olson and Strauss, 1984; Rovee-Collier, 1984; Werner and Perlmutter, 1979).

Memory in the Second Six Months
after Birth

Many 10-month-olds can crawl, stand, and understand some words. Compared to a 3- or 4-month-old, the 10-month-old seems very grown up indeed. In particular, the older infant is acquiring the motor and verbal skills that allow her to explore and understand her environment much more extensively than was possible just a few months previously. These advances occur in memory as well. Some basic recognitory skills emerge in the first six months; in the next six months these skills become elaborated to provide the first inkling of the memory skills of childhood that were the focus of Chapters 2 to 4.

The Emergence of Recall. Many theorists distinguish recognition memory from recall memory (e.g., Anderson and Bower, 1972; Bahrick, 1970). Recognition memory is usually thought to be the less complex of the two. In recognition, a stimulus is present physically and the subject must merely decide if it is familiar or not; in recall, the stimulus is absent and must be retrieved from memory.

Recognitory skill is present at birth and develops considerably in the first six months. The onset of recall is more difficult to specify: Among adults and verbal children, the usual procedure is to present a set of stimuli to be remembered, remove the stimuli, and then ask the subject to recall the set. Giving comparable instructions to an infant with limited verbal skill is not easy. One source of evidence concerning recall is infants' search for objects. By 7 months, infants will look for objects that are out of sight (Ashmead and Perlmutter, 1980). For example, if a toy is placed directly in front of an infant, then covered with a cloth, 7-month-olds will retrieve the toy successfully, but 5- and 6-month-olds will not (Fox, Kagan, and Weiskopf, 1979). Requiring an infant to wait briefly seems to disrupt memory considerably. At 8 months, a delay of any sort makes it impossible for the infant to find a toy that has been placed under one of two identical cloths (Szpak, cited in Fox, Kagan, and Weiskopf, 1979). But by 10 months, infants can wait as long as seven seconds and still find the hidden object successfully. By 16 to 18 months, recall is still possible after delays of 20 to 30 seconds (Daehler, Bukatko, Benson, and Myers, 1976; Hunter, 1913, 1917).

These studies probably underestimate infants' recall, for the hiding locations are quite similar with few distinguishing cues. Consistent with this view is work by DeLoache and Brown (1979, 1983). In these studies, 20- and 27-month-olds were shown a toy— either Mickey Mouse or Big Bird—that the child watched being hidden somewhere in the house, perhaps in a desk drawer or behind a pillow. After intervals ranging from three minutes to overnight, even younger children found the toy on more than half of the hidings.

The assumption in all of these studies is that children's search for the hidden object is based on their ability to recall the experience of seeing the now-absent toy hidden. Much the same assumption is used to infer recall from studies of *imitation*. Here an infant sees an experimenter perform a sequence of actions with some toys. The toys are then given to the infant, who may play with them in his own way, or—more interestingly, for our purposes—may decide to repeat the experimenter's actions.

McCall, Parke, and Kavanaugh (1977) examined infants' ability to imitate 14 separate behaviors. For one, the experimenter drew a line and several dots on a pad. For another, the experimenter placed a screen in front of her face, then played peek-a-boo with the infant. After the experimenter had modeled a behavior twice, the objects used were placed directly in front of the infant. The 12-month-olds imitated motor acts (e.g., drawing lines and dots) perfectly approximately 30 percent of the time and social acts (e.g., playing peek-a-boo) 20 percent of the time. These figures increased to 75 and 45 percent for 24-month-olds.

McCall, Parke, and Kavanaugh (1977) also examined delayed imitation: Several minutes later each object was presented a second time. Delayed imitation was much less likely for all acts and at all ages. For example, 12-month-olds imitated only 7 percent of the motor acts and 24-month-olds imitated 19 percent.

Imitation and search for hidden objects are indirect measures of recall. In particular, the absence of imitation and the failure to find a hidden object does not imply that infants lack the capacity to recall. Infants may not imitate because they prefer to play with objects in other ways or because the experimenter's actions are too complex for the infants' motor skill level. Hence, we are probably being quite conservative in concluding that the ability to recall prior experiences emerges in the middle of the first year and increases gradually thereafter.

Cognitive "Economy." Children, adolescents, and adults often "economize" their memories of experiences; instead of remembering each specific experience, they create a mental representation that preserves and integrates the important features of those experiences. These representations are based upon a person's knowledge of those experiences (i.e., the example in Chapter 4 concerning inferences based on knowledge of baseball).

Between 6 and 12 months, infants learn about a large number of categories, including animals, food, vehicles, quantities, and furniture (Olson and Strauss, 1984). Infants start to respond to stimuli as members of conceptual categories, not merely as individual stimuli. Older infants, for example, realize that *car* refers to a class of objects, not simply to one specific vehicle.

As we saw in Chapter 4, such knowledge can distort children's memory, in that memory for specific instances is biased in the direction of the expected or typical experience. Strauss (1979) has shown that the same kinds of distortions occur in infants' retention. To understand the logic behind Strauss' study, imagine this: During the first day in a new school, a 14-year-old asks ten students their favorite sport and their favorite school subject. The outcome of her informal poll is shown in Table 5-1. Asked to describe a typical student in her new school, she would be likely to say, "Kids seem to like football and math" (e.g., Hayes-Roth and Hayes-Roth, 1977). From Table 5-1, though, we see how bias toward the most frequent experience can distort memories. Football and math were mentioned most often, but not together; not a single individual liked football *and* math. Instead, the most frequently co-occuring preferences were *baseball* and math (three students, Ben, Gay, and Jeff). What this 14-year-old remembered was a mythical "average student" who corresponded to no person she had actually met.

Table 5-1 Students and their Preferences

Student's Name	Favorite Sport	Favorite School Subject
Alex	Football	Math
Ben	Baseball	Math
Cynthia	Basketball	Math
Dan	Football	English
Ellen	Football	English
Fran	Basketball	Math
Gay	Baseball	Math
Harold	Football	Science
Ilene	Football	English
Jeff	Baseball	Math

Strauss (1979) showed that 10-month-olds remember experiences through a similar sort of averaging process: Infants viewed each of 14 different faces for five seconds. Recognition tests followed that paired various types of faces. The key findings concern a previously unseen face that was the average of the 14 presented faces. That is, this face was the average of the 14 in terms of the length and width of the nose, the length of the head, and the separation of the eyes. Infants treated this face as familiar—looked at it less—when it was paired with (1) a completely novel face, or (2) a face with features from the 14 previous faces that were not average features. Infants' memory for the 14 faces corresponded to no particular face that they had actually seen; instead they remembered a space-saving composite of the 14 faces.

In this study, as well as in the example of the student's new friends, we set up contrived conditions so that memory distortions would be particularly likely to occur. This apparent trickery should not imply that this aspect of memory is maladaptive. Integration of successive experiences allows a person to create a mental summary of the gist of those experiences. As Strauss and Carter (1984) point out, "This ability may be especially important for the . . . infant who is constantly being confronted with novel environmental information." (p. 320)

Memories of Infancy and Early Childhood

A few weeks ago, my 5-year-old son started kindergarten. Listening to him describe his day's activities, I tried to remember my own experiences in kindergarten. I could remember that the room had a large bay window; I remember once coming home from school in someone's convertible; I recall counting past 100 while walking home from school. I could recall little else from kindergarten and essentially nothing of my life that occurred prior to kindergarten.

This inability to remember events from early in one's life, known as *infantile amnesia*, is not unique to me, nor for that matter to humans. To the contrary, all humans experience infantile amnesia to some degree, as do dogs, foxes, rats, mice and frogs (Spear, 1979). The data in Figure 5-5, from Waldfogel (1948), were obtained by asking undergraduates to recall any experiences that occurred prior to their eighth birthday. They were also asked to state their age at the time of the experience. These individuals recalled almost no experiences prior to their third birthday. Most individuals remembered a few events from ages 3 to 5 years, with retention increasing steadily thereafter.

This pattern does not change when individuals are asked about a single important event from child-

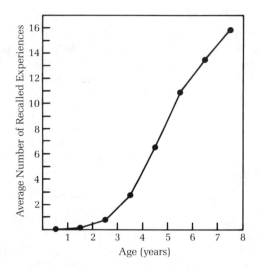

Figure 5-5   *Average number of experiences recalled by adults as a function of their age at the time of the experience.* [Data from Waldfogel (1948).]

hood. Sheingold and Tenney (1982) asked undergraduates a series of questions about the birth of a younger sibling. Among the questions were (1) "Who told you that your mother was leaving to go to the hospital?" (2) "How did you find out that the baby was a boy or girl?" (3) "Did you visit your mother while she was in the hospital?" If subjects were younger than 3 years old at the time of the sibling's birth, they typically recalled nothing of the event. Some aspects of the birth were first recalled when the subject was 3 years old at the time, and recall improved steadily from that age on.

An obvious shortcoming in these data is the difficulty in determining the accuracy of subjects' recall and, in the Waldfogel (1948) study, the accuracy with which subjects estimated their age at the time of the experience. Fortunately, other investigators (e.g., Dudycha and Dudycha, 1933; Gold and Neisser, 1980) have been able to determine—with varying degrees of precision—the experiences and the age of the individual at the time of the experiences. The profile of infantile amnesia from these studies is much the same.

Infantile amnesia does not simply reflect poor retention after a longer period of time: Readers born prior to 1957 or 1958 almost certainly recall with extraordinary precision what they were doing when told that President John F. Kennedy had been shot in Dallas, an event that occurred more than 20 years ago (Brown and Kulik, 1977).* Similarly, 65-year-olds typically recall the names of as many as 20 high school classmates, even though nearly 50 years have elapsed since graduation (Bahrick, Bahrick, and Wittlinger, 1975). It is not, then, simply the passage of much time that complicates recall of early experiences. Something about the fact that they occur early in life makes them less accessible to us as adults.

Explanations for infantile amnesia abound (Spear, 1979, 1984; White and Pillemer, 1979). The first came from Freud (1905/1953) who noticed infantile amnesia in his early work in psychoanalysis. For Freud, amnesia represented repression. Due to the sexual nature of many early experiences, the entire period was "shut off" from other recollections. Freud (1905/1953) described it as an "... amnesia similar to that which neurotics exhibit for later events, and of which the essence consists in a single withholding of these impressions from consciousness ..." (p. 175).

*I was in an eighth-grade English class, in the second row of seats from the window, four or five seats from the front. The teacher was Mrs. Witte and Carolyn Itce was sitting directly in front of me. The announcement came over a loudspeaker mounted above the door on the right side of the room.

When cast in contemporary terms, Freud's explanation is essentially one of *retrieval failure*. The experiences are still represented in memory, but the individual cannot gain access to them.

There are two other general explanations of infantile amnesia. One possibility is that it is not the unique phenomenon that it appears to be. Retention is determined, in part, by the quality and degree of original learning of the experience. Younger individuals may not store experiences as elaborately as do older individuals; hence these experiences are forgotten more rapidly. Another possibility is that younger and older organisms store experiences in memory in exactly the same way, but some factors associated with early development disrupt those stored representations; they are "lost" thereafter.

Only recently have these three hypotheses—inadequate storage, disrupted storage, and retrieval failure—been evaluated. The relevant work has been done exclusively with nonhuman subjects, for the nature of the experimentation makes it impossible to do with humans. The state of the art is such that we cannot pinpoint one hypothesis as the likely source of infantile amnesia (Spear, 1984); instead, I will illustrate the logic of the experimentation used to evaluate each hypothesis.

First, consider the possibility of inadequate storage. The strategy here is first to be sure that animals of different ages learn an experience comparably, and then to examine their subsequent retention. According to the hypothesis of inadequate storage in young animals, infantile amnesia should be eliminated when original learning is equated for animals of different ages. Feigley and Spear (1970, Experiment 1), for example, trained young (21- to 25-day-old) and adult (60- to 85-day-old) rats to jump across a barrier

to avoid electric shock.* The two groups did not differ in the rate at which they learned to jump over the
barrier; nevertheless, 28 days later the young rats had
completely forgotten the contingency between jumping and shock but adult rats had not.

   This finding would appear to discredit explanation of infantile amnesia in terms of inadequate storage, yet this may not be the case. Feigley and Spear
(1970) found young and adult rats to be equal in terms
of one index of learning—the number of trials needed
to achieve a criterion of five consecutive, successful
jumps to avoid shock. This is surely a plausible measure of learning, but not the only one. One could just as
plausibly measure how quickly rats jump when they
are given a signal that shock is imminent. To completely rule out the hypothesis of inadequate storage,
one would have to demonstrate poorer retention by
younger organisms when they have been equated
with older animals for all possible measures of learning—a time-consuming and possibly impossible en-
deavor (Potash and Ferguson, 1977; Spear and
Kucharski, 1984).

   Next consider the hypothesis that infantile amnesia reflects disrupted storage of an experience. If
this explanation is correct, then infantile amnesia
should be reduced or eliminated if we prevent the
occurrence of the disruptive events. Smith and Spear
(1981, Experiment 1) showed how this might occur.
Young and adult rats learned to enter one arm of a
T-maze to avoid electric shock. The animals differed
in their experiences prior to learning. Some animals

---

*Some milestones may be useful to readers unfamiliar with the normal
development of *Rattus norvegicus*, the traditional laboratory white rat. At
birth its eyes and ears are closed. The ears open at 12 or 13 days; the eyes,
at 14 or 15 days. It is usually weaned at 21 days and achieves sexual
maturity at 50 to 60 days.

had no prior experience in the apparatus; others had experience in which shocks were administered in a different-shaped apparatus. Animals in three other groups had various experiences in the apparatus by which they learned to avoid shock.

Prior experience had a negligible (beneficial) impact on learning, for both young and adult rats. The interesting results concern retention. Seven days after the learning experience, young rats with prior experience in the apparatus had completely forgotten the avoidance response; young rats with no prior experience or experience in another apparatus remembered the response almost perfectly. Prior experience had no impact on adults' retention. It is almost as if, for young but not adult rats, what were once distinct memories of separate experiences in an apparatus "intermingled" over time.

A possible reason for this "intermingling" of memories is that radical changes occur in the rat's central nervous system between 15 and 30 days of age. For example, neurotransmitters in the brain become more concentrated and the number of synapses in the cerebral cortex increases by a factor of ten (Spear, 1979). As these changes occur, records of previous experiences may become distorted.

This explanation does lead to a simple prediction: Infantile amnesia should be reduced in species whose central nervous systems are relatively mature at birth. The guinea pig is such a species, and in fact it does not exhibit infantile amnesia: Campbell, Misanin, White, and Lytle (1974) trained thirsty guinea pigs to avoid an electric shock by *not* drinking from a spout. Guinea pigs trained at 2 and 3 days of age remembered this contingency just as accurately 42 days later as did adults.

In the final hypothesis, infantile amnesia is due to retrieval failure. Experiences that are stored and retained successfully are somehow inaccessible, much as a locked room is inaccessible without a key. One of the most frequently suggested causes of this retrieval failure is a change in the contextual cues that are available to guide retrieval. Generally, recall is most likely when the context of recall is exactly the same as the context of original learning (e.g., Tulving and Thomson, 1973). But the "context" of infancy differs radically from the "context" of later life. Adults interpret many experiences via language, something that infants rarely do. Infants experience frequent physical contact; adults do not.

According to the retrieval failure account, infantile amnesia would be reduced if adults re-experienced contexts from infancy. Tomkins (1970), for one, suggested

In order to retrieve childhood memories, we should . . . fabricate rooms from two to two-and-one-half times normal linear size in all dimensions. The oversized house and rooms should contain furniture, drapery, and accessories to scale . . . in an oversized crib, we might place the adult clothed only in oversized diapers, surrounded by oversized blocks, looked down upon by a huge face of a giantess mother with a loud, booming high fidelity voice emitting sweet nothings as she gazed at our subject, pinched, tweaked, poked, and fondled him, and from time to time fed him milk from a very large bottle. (pp. 108–109)

Obviously we cannot do this experiment literally, with either humans or rats. We could, however, remind the organism of a previous context, using the reinstatement procedures described earlier in this chapter. That is, young rats could be reminded of an early experience, at a time when they ordinarily would have forgotten the experience. When this is done, for instance by placing rats in a maze and shocking them briefly, infantile amnesia is eliminated (e.g., Coulter, 1979; Haroutunian and Riccio, 1979; Richardson, Ebner, and Riccio, 1981).

I have described three potential explanations for infantile amnesia and illustrated the research strategies that are designed to examine each. Everything is not as pat as it may appear here; there is counterevidence for each of the findings described. As Spear (1984) noted, "Infantile amnesia is a problem for which plausible theories far outnumber substantial facts" (p. 327). Perhaps most important at this point is to realize that infantile amnesia, however mysterious it may have seemed when first described by Freud, is certainly capable of being understood in terms of the basic memory processes that have been discussed throughout this book.

Summary

Our intuitions about the importance of experiences early in life presuppose that infants have at least minimal memory skills. One such skill, recognition of stimuli seen or heard previously, has been demonstrated with newborns using the habituation paradigm. This paradigm has also been used to demonstrate retention for up to two weeks in 6-month-olds. A conjugate reinforcement paradigm, in which an infant's kicks move a mobile, leads to longer estimates of retention for 2- and 3-month-olds. In both paradigms, however, memory improves between 2 and 6 months of age. These improvements may reflect the fact that older infants (1) encode stimuli more

elaborately than younger ones, (2) are more successful at retrieving information they have already stored,
or (3) both.

We first see precursors of some childhood memory skills beginning at 6 months. Using hiding tasks,
recall memory is detected at 6 or 7 months. It improves substantially in the ensuing 18 months, based
on work with hiding tasks and imitation. A second
memory milestone from this period is that infants
begin to "economize"—they construct general representations of experience that integrate the important
features of individual experiences.

These experiences from infancy cannot be recalled in adulthood, a phenomenon known as infantile amnesia. Occurring in developing humans and
nonhumans alike, infantile amnesia is thought to be
due to one (or more) of the following: (1) young organisms store experiences less adequately than older
organisms; (2) experiences are stored adequately but
lost during development; and (3) the stored experience is intact during adulthood but cannot be retrieved, probably because the contextual cues that
guide retrieval ordinarily change radically between
infancy and adulthood.

Detailed analyses of these factors is just underway. Currently some research—all done with nonhuman organisms—points to each as a causal factor.
Notably, each factor represents the application of a
general principle of memory to the particular setting
of early development, not an explanation unique to
infantile amnesia.

6

Memory in Mentally Retarded Children

Rosemary was a pretty baby girl, and it was only slowly, as she grew to be a toddler and beyond, that I began to realize she might be handicapped.

She was slow in everything, and some things she seemed unable to learn how to do, or do well or with consistency. . . . She went to kindergarten and first grade at the usual ages, but her lack of coordination was apparent and as time went on I realized she could not keep up with the work. In the Brookline school system intelligence tests were given to all the children very early. I was informed that Rosemary's I.Q. was very low, but that was about all the concrete information I received, and it didn't help much. This was in the early 1920s, the tests were still quite new and unrefined, and neither those who created them nor those who used them could say, really, how accurate they were or what the scores meant except in a general way . . . when I would ask, "What can I do to help her?" there didn't seem to be much of an answer. I was frustrated and heartbroken. (Kennedy, 1974, pp. 151–152)

This passage, taken from Rose Fitzgerald Kennedy's autobiography, expresses the sentiments of many parents of retarded children. Their children do not learn easily and the parents seek help. Fortunately, the situation has improved since the 1920s. Now we know a great deal about the cognitive skills of mentally retarded individuals. Based on this understanding, it is now possible to improve the learning and memory skills of these people.

Before turning to research on learning and memory, a few comments are necessary on mental retardation per se. First, the term *retardation* literally means to slow down or delay. Accordingly, implicit in the term mental retardation—as opposed to a term such as mental deficiency, for example—is the view that mentally retarded people follow essentially the same sequence of intellectual development as do nonretarded people, only at a much slower rate. One implication of this view is that mentally retarded individuals will rarely perform like nonretarded children of the same chronological age, but will more often perform like younger children who are their intellectual peers. In fact, much of this chapter will focus on retarded adolescents whose mental age is 6 to 8 years, and whose cognitive abilities resemble those of nonretarded 6- and 8-year-olds. These similarities are so widespread—at least in the intellectual domain—that research on young, nonretarded children is often used to generate hypotheses about cognitive functioning in retarded individuals, and vice-versa (Borkowski and Cavanaugh, 1979; Brown, 1978).

It is also important to point out that the population of mentally retarded people is extraordinarily heterogeneous. Traditionally, a mentally retarded person is one whose IQ score is below 70 (with the majority of humans falling between 80 and 120). Individuals with IQ scores between 55 and 70 are often referred to as mildly retarded, or as the *educable mentally retarded*. These individuals typically attend public schools, though they need special attention of some form. At the other extreme are profoundly retarded individuals, whose IQ scores are less than 25. As adults these people are often unable to talk intelligibly or to walk, and some may not be toilet trained.

In addition to variability in degree of retardation, the basis for retardation varies. In some mentally retarded individuals, their abnormal intellectual skills can be traced to damage of some sort to the central nervous system. For other individuals, no such damage can be identified.

Obviously, it makes little sense to talk about memory in the mentally retarded as if they were a uniform group of individuals. Instead, we need to study memory in well-defined subgroups of retarded people. In this chapter, we begin by discussing research on memory in the educable mentally retarded, where the emphasis has been on teaching retarded people to use memory strategies. Next, we turn to a very different population, the profoundly retarded. Here questions are simpler and answers harder to come by, for retardation is so extreme that measuring cognitive functioning at all has, until recently, been an elusive aim. In the third section of this chapter we discuss a special group of retarded persons called *idiot savants* who are thought to have exceptional memory skills.

Memory in Educable Retarded Children

Our views on memory functioning in educable retarded persons have changed in the past 20 years. Ellis (1963) proposed one of the first explanations of the memory deficit in retarded children. He suggested that memory traces decay more rapidly in retarded than in nonretarded persons. If rate of decay is more rapid in retarded persons, then memory differences between retarded and nonretarded children should increase as the retention interval increases, as shown in Figure 6.1. This pattern of results was not found often, and, when it did emerge, it seemed to reflect differences in the extent to which children used effective strategies to learn the material initially, rather than differences in rate of decay per se (Belmont and Butterfield, 1969). This latter observation, in turn, prompted a new flurry of studies designed to show that retarded and nonretarded children differ in the likelihood and success with which they use mnemonic strategies. These investigations have proved most fruitful, as it is now accepted that one basis for memory deficits in the educable mentally retarded is found in their failure to use strategies appropriately (Belmont and Butterfield, 1971; Brown, 1974). That is, the mentally retarded child, like the preschool and young school-age child, does not seem to engage in the sort of planful behavior typical of adults and older children.

The description here of research on training memory skills of educable mentally retarded individuals will be very selective; the research literature is large and growing, and we can devote but a few pages to it. The interested reader should see chapters by Belmont and Butterfield (1977), Borkowski and Cavanaugh (1979), and Campione and Brown (1977) for more information on training memory skills in retarded persons. Also, a book edited by Ellis (1979) contains a number of useful chapters, as does the series *International Review of Research in Mental Retardation*.

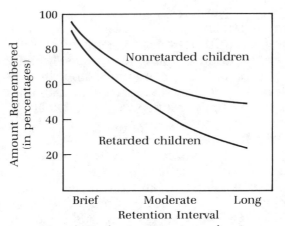

Figure 6-1 *Hypothetical retention curves showing amount of information retained a function of the length of the retention interval, plotted separately for retarded and nonretarded children.*

Spontaneous Use of Strategies

Instances in which retarded children fail to use mnemonic strategies or use them inappropriately or ineffectively are numerous. Two studies demonstrate the point clearly. Belmont and Butterfield (1971) studied retarded people's use of rehearsal. Retarded and nonretarded adolescents were tested on a serial-position recall task. A series of letters was presented; then a duplicate of one of the letters appeared, and subjects indicated the location of the letter in the series. Nonretarded adolescents recalled letters from the beginning of the series quite accurately, a level of performance that presumably reflects their skilled use of rehearsal. In contrast, retarded adolescents' recall of items from the beginning of the list was uniformly low, suggesting the absence of rehearsal.

Rehearsal is most appropriate when the amount of information to be remembered is small. As the amount of information increases, mnemonics that organize the information to be remembered become more appropriate. Such organizational strategies have been studied by asking children to remember several words from each of a few different categories. We might ask a child to remember *pants, orange, car, shirt, plane, shoes, blue, boat, green*. A likely result would be that a child recalls *pants, shoes, orange, green, blue, boat, plane*. Although retention is not perfect, the child has used the categories—clothing, colors, vehicles—to organize recall.

Retarded individuals seem to use this sort of organizing scheme less frequently than nonretarded individuals, just as preschool and school-age children are less likely to do so than older children. This finding has been documented in a series of studies by Spitz (1966). In one study, for example, retarded and nonretarded adolescents were asked to remember 20 words, with 5 words presented from each of four categories. Words were presented in a random order. Rarely did retarded persons recall words from a category in succession, which would have suggested the use of an organizational strategy.

Training Retarded Individuals to Use Strategies

These studies by Belmont and Butterfield (1971) and Spitz (1966) are representative of many in which retarded children are found to be unlikely to use mnemonics in laboratory memory tasks. Having identified one source of memory deficit in retarded people, a logical next step is to determine if we can improve retention through training, perhaps even to the level of nonretarded peers. This turns out to be a more complex task than it might first appear, because of several difficulties involved in evaluating the success of a training program. Three criteria are particularly relevant. We would first want to consider the *durability* of training. Retarded children can be taught to rehearse (e.g., Belmont and Butterfield, 1971), with improved retention as a consequence, but if we tested these children a week later and the effects of training had vanished, then our initial finding of improved rehearsal would be trivial. Consequently, we want to be sure that training results in some long-lasting changes in retarded children's memory.

Assuming training had met the criterion of durability, we would next want to consider the extent to which the retarded children could *generalize* their newly acquired skills to situations different from those in which they were learned. If the skill is limited to a particular set of stimuli presented by a particular experimenter in a particular context, then the value of the training should be questioned. If we find that retarded children are using rehearsal to remember the events planned for a day, or what to buy at the market, then the program would seem to have potential merit.

A final point that we would wish to consider would be the extent to which retarded and nonretarded individuals differ in their memory skills after the retarded individuals have been trained. The most stringent criterion for a program would be the elimination of memory differences between retarded and nonretarded subjects. As programs fall further from this goal, their success becomes more open to question.

With these three criteria—durability, generalization, and minimization of retardate-nonretardate differences—we are in a better position to evaluate studies in which the goal was to improve retarded individuals' memory.

From the results of a study by Brown, Campione, and Murphy (1974), it is clear that the goal of durability can be achieved. These investigators taught retarded children to rehearse. After an interval of six months, the subjects were retested without further instruction or reference to their earlier training. The effects of training were as evident after six months as they had been immediately following instruction. Similar results come from a study by Burger, Blackman, and Tan (1980) in which retarded adolescents were trained to organize information in conceptual categories. Tested six months later, these individuals used the strategy with the same proficiency as immediately following training.

Of course, not all training efforts achieve the durability described here (e.g., Jensen and Rohwer, 1963). One of the key factors that determine the degree of maintenance is the amount of training. Often a very brief training session can improve a retarded person's use of strategies, but maintenance is not attained. Apparently, training needs to continue until individuals use the strategy nearly perfectly (Borkowski and Cavanaugh, 1979). That is, rudimentary training will often improve recall substantially, but to achieve maintenance, additional training is needed to allow subjects to "fine tune" their use of strategies.

Training programs do not fare as well against the criterion of generalization (Campione and Brown, 1977). The fragility of training can be seen by returning to the study of Brown, Campione, and Murphy (1974), which demonstrated impressive durability of training. Later, these retarded individuals were tested on another memory task for which rehearsal was again the appropriate strategy. Their performance was indistinguishable from a control group of retarded subjects who had received no training. Rehearsal training seemed to be linked specifically to a particular context.

What additional training is necessary to achieve generalization? One idea stems from the diagnosis-treatment-monitoring sequence described in Chapter 3. In all of the studies described thus far, the training has involved the treatment phase of this sequence; the diagnosis and monitoring phases have been ignored entirely. The likely consequences of such training become evident if we pursue the medical analogy a bit. Suppose a physician were given extensive training in treating some form of cancer, but she were taught only one symptom. If other, relevant, symptoms were present, the physician would not "generalize" (i.e., prescribe the treatment) because she would not recognize those symptoms as calling for exactly the same treatment. The training given to retarded persons in previous studies may lead to a similar type of "tunnel vision" in which the trained strategy is associated with a very specific task and goal rather than being recognized as a general skill to be applied widely.

Consistent with this view is research indicating that retarded people are not skilled at the diagnostic phase of mnemonic problem-solving. For example, retarded people are very poor at estimating the difficulty of memory problems (e.g., Brown, Campione, and Murphy, 1977).

This analysis of the problem contains the seed of a solution. Medical students learn that multiple symptoms can point to a common diagnosis and treatment; perhaps retarded individuals should be taught the mnemonic equivalent. "Instead of training a routine that is specifically tailored to the needs of a specific task, it might be useful to inculcate more general knowledge concerning strategies and their use and control" (Brown, Campione, and Barclay, 1979, p. 502).

Beginning in the late 1970s, several studies were conducted in which investigators examined the impact of training both a specific strategy and a general understanding of that strategy (e.g., Belmont, Butterfield, and Borkowski, 1978; Brown, Campione, and Barclay, 1979; Kendall, Borkowski, and Cavanaugh, 1980; Kramer and Engle 1981). A study of Belmont, Butterfield, and Borkowski (1978) illustrates the nature of this type of training and its impact on memory. Their approach was to teach some retarded adolescents one method of memorizing, and other retarded adolescents two versions of essentially the same method. Belmont, Butterfield, and Borkowski (1978) reasoned that if subjects were shown that the strategy could be modified to fit different tasks, they would be more likely to modify the strategy spontaneously in the future. The task was to recall seven letters. Presentation was paced by the subject: Letters were presented in succession, but the subject could study each individual letter for an unlimited amount of time. Following study of the seventh letter, the subject was to recall the last three letters in their order of presentation, followed by the first four letters in order.

All subjects were trained to use a "cumulative rehearsal–fast finish" method, rehearsing the first four letters aloud, then looking at the last three letters very briefly. Training was very effective: Subjects recalled nearly 50 percent of the letters, compared to only 20 percent prior to training.

Belmont, Butterfield, and Borkowski (1978) next

modified the recall requirements of the task, asking subjects to recall the last four letters in order, then the first three. Half of the subjects were then

treated to a thorough discussion of how, first of all, a fast-finish is much more difficult with 4 letters than with 3, so a little repetition of those 4 terminal letters is appropriate; but . . . the rehearsal of the early 3 letters is easier than the previous 4-letter rehearsal. By such comparisons we tried to have the child understand the harmony of input and output processes, and the similarities and differences between the cumulative-rehearsal–fast-finish method for the [two] . . . tasks. (p. 421)

In short, Belmont, Butterfield, and Borkowski (1978) trained their subjects in the art of selecting a strategy based on a sound diagnosis of the problem.

Subsequently, subjects were given a key test of generalization. The recall requirements were changed again, so that the subject recalled the last two letters in order, then the first five. Consider first the subjects who had received only the original training on rehearsal: These subjects did not rehearse at all and, predictably, their recall was very poor. In contrast, those individuals given additional training on diagnosis rehearsed skillfully and their recall on the generalization task was essentially as accurate as directly after training.

These findings, then, indicate that retarded people will be most likely to generalize a newly learned strategy if they understand some of the reasons why the strategy works and, hence, when it is most effective. Of course, training these companion diagnostic skills is not always as simple as it was in the Belmont, Butterfield, and Borkowski (1978) study; as yet we are just beginning to understand the type of diagnostic training needed to foster general understanding of more complex strategies (e.g., Brown, Campione, and Barclay, 1979).

The final criterion for evaluation of training programs is the extent to which retarded-nonretarded differences in memory are reduced or eliminated. In training studies of the type described here, differences are consistently reduced by an impressive amount, but they are almost never eliminated. What processes are responsible for this residual memory deficit? This is a more difficult question to answer than we might first suspect because differences between retarded and nonretarded people may reflect our failure to adequately train rather than an inherent deficiency in the retarded person's memory. That is, after much additional training, perhaps involving months or years, we could conceivably eliminate all memory differences between retarded and nonretarded persons. Furthermore, motivational factors may account for part of the difference that remains after training (e.g., Zigler, 1969).

Recognition Memory

One memory task that reveals the retarded individual's juxtaposition of mnemonic strengths and weaknesses is recognition memory. Retarded people are often essentially as accurate as nonretarded people on recognition memory tasks (e.g., Brown, 1972; Ellis, McCartney, Ferretti, and Cavalier, 1977). A quite different picture emerges when we consider another aspect of performance in recognition; namely, the speed with which memory is searched to determine if an item is familiar. Evidence from a memory search paradigm introduced by Sternberg (1966) indicates that retarded people are consistently slower in their search of memory than nonretarded people. In

Sternberg's (1966) procedure, a child is asked to re-member a brief list of digits: say, 1, 5, and 2. Then a single digit is shown, and the child is asked to deter-mine as quickly as possible if the digit is a member of the set shown immediately before. Of particular in-terest is the relation of the speed with which the child answers and the number of digits in the list the child was to remember. For each additional digit that must be remembered, nonretarded children's reaction time typically increases by approximately 40 to 50 milli-seconds. This value represents the amount of time necessary to search memory for each additional digit.

Differences between retarded and nonretarded children in speed of memory search have been found in two studies in which this paradigm was used. Dugas and Kellas (1974) compared the performance of retarded adolescents with a group of fifth- and sixth-graders. Memory search times of the normal children increased 45 milliseconds for every addi-tional digit in the set; retarded adolescents' search times increased nearly twice as much, approximately 90 milliseconds.

Similar findings were reported in a more elabo-rate experiment by Harris and Fleer (1974). Four groups of subjects were tested. Two groups of re-tarded subjects, both with mean IQs of 56, differed in etiology. One consisted of children whose retardation could be traced directly to brain damage (e.g., prena-tal injury). Children in the second group were cultur-al-familial retardates, a term indicating classification based solely on intelligence test scores and social factors, with no evidence of organic damage. Two groups of nonretarded people were also tested. A group of 8-year-olds matched the retarded subjects in mental age, and a group of high school students matched them in chronological age.

For both 8-year-olds and high school students, the increase in memory search was approximately 40 milliseconds for every additional digit. Values were larger for the retarded adolescents. The increase was 66 milliseconds for the cultural-familial group and 111 milliseconds for the brain-damaged individuals. Thus, both Dugas and Kellas (1974) and Harris and Fleer (1974) found that memory search was slower in retarded people. The estimates of retarded subjects memory search speed differ between the two studies, but this is probably due to the fact that Dugas and Kellas apparently selected subjects without regard to etiology. Consistent with this explanation, the average of the search times for Harris and Fleer's two groups of the retarded subjects is 88 milliseconds, almost exactly the value obtained by Dugas and Kellas.

Recognition in Profoundly Retarded Persons

The educable mentally retarded people described in the previous section often lead productive lives, holding a job and having a family. The prognosis is not so optimistic for profoundly retarded individuals. They require constant care to survive, with the practical result that these individuals spend most of their lives in institutions. They usually do not walk unaided and have limited speech (if, indeed, they learn to talk at all).

For these individuals, a principal difficulty has long been to determine precisely the extent of their disability. The problem has been the lack of a response by which memory and other cognitive processes may be measured. Because the individuals have limited motor and verbal skills, most of the traditional measures of memory are inapppropriate. The problem we face in assessing memory in profoundly retarded individuals, then, is much the same situation encountered in studying infants' memory. This similarity suggests a solution to the problem, one that reseachers first used in the middle 1970s. Specifically, memory paradigms devised for infants are adapted for use with profoundly retarded children.

Consider a study by Shepherd and Fagan (1981). They tested profoundly retarded 7-year-olds, whose average mental age was only 4 months. The paradigm was essentially the same as that used by Fagan (1970, 1973) to study recognition memory in normal 6-month-old infants: Children saw one stimulus for 30 seconds, then saw that stimulus paired with a novel stimulus for 10 seconds. On the recognition test, these children looked at the novel stimulus for 60 percent of the time, a finding that suggests that the children recognized the familiar stimulus. (See Chapter 5 for a review of the rationale underlying the habituation procedure and pitfalls associated with it.)

Butcher (1977) used the same general approach to study immediate and delayed recognition. The profoundly retarded children in her sample had an average chronological age of 6 years and an average mental age of 5 months. Children saw a stimulus—either a photograph of a face or a colored pattern—for two minutes; on a recognition test that stimulus was paired with a novel one. When the recognition test immediately followed the study trial, children looked at the novel stimulus 62 percent of the time. However, when the recognition test was delayed by only 40 seconds, children looked equally long at the novel and familiar stimuli. This inability to recognize stimuli after a brief interval contrasts sharply, of course, with the recognition skills of nonretarded 6-year-olds. More important is the fact that the retarded children's delayed recognition skill falls below that of their intellectual peers, nonretarded 5-month-olds. Recall, from Chapter 5, that 5- and 6-month-olds recognize a face for up to *two weeks* following two minutes of study.

Unfortunately, little else can be said about memory in profoundly retarded individuals (see Shepherd and Fagan, 1981, for a review), for research is really just getting underway. We are far from a point at which research will suggest ways to improve the cognitive abilities of these people.

The Strange Case of the Idiot Savant

From clinical cases, we have many examples of children with extraordinary memory skills. Perhaps the most interesting class of such individuals are the so-called idiot savants. A precise definition of the idiot savant has proven elusive, but the term is generally used to refer to an individual who is considerably below average on all measures of ability save one, in which he or she has extraordinary proficiency (Hill, 1978). Jones (1926), for example described K, a 38-year-old man with a mental age of 11 years who could name the population of every town in the United States with a population greater than 5000. Furthermore, doing so usually took three seconds or less. He used this and other esoteric knowledge to remember long strings of digits. Asked how he remembered the digits *4836179621*, K reported:

When I saw the number I read it as *4, 836, 179, 621.* I remembered 4 because of the 4th of July. *836* I just had to memorize, without any help, but if I were doing it again it would probably occur to me that *836* was the Chinese population of the state of Texas in 1910, and then I wouldn't forget it. *179* is easy to remember because that is the number of miles from New York to Harrisburg, and *621* is the number of a house I know in Denver, Colorado. (p. 372)

Idiot savants have achieved notoriety for several skills, but most frequently their abilities have related to musical talent, speed in arithmetic, or knowledge of the calendar. The latter group of children, sometimes called "calendar calculators," is of interest here, because this skill seems to be dependent to a very great extent on mnemonic processing. Consider, for example, the case of L, an 11-year-old boy whose IQ was reported as 50 and who was unable to learn in school or interact socially. Yet he could name the day of the week for any date between the years of 1880 and 1950 (Scheerer, Rothman, and Goldstein, 1945).

Two questions concerning the exceptional abilities of L and other idiot savants are relevant here. First, what are the mechanisms underlying their expert performance? Second, what factors led to the development of the exceptional talent? With regard to the processes involved in the performance of idiot savants on calendar calculations, a large dose of rote memorization seems to be involved, at least initially. From the case reports, it is clear that, for unknown reasons, dates of the calendar had a particular attraction for many idiot savants from an early age. For example, George was a 24-year-old with an IQ in the 60 to 70 range whose knowledge of the calendar was essentially perfect between the years 1 and 40400. As a child, he spent hours at a time examining the family almanac (Horwitz, Deming, and Winter, 1969). His parents noted George's fascination with the almanac and gave him a perpetual calendar to encourage his interest. Similarly, as a 6-year-old, L began keeping track of special days, such as birthdays and the day he last saw an individual. Apparently as a consquence of this early, intense interest in the calendar, both George and L committed the dates of many years to memory.

Rote memorization of a portion of the calendar is indispensable, but many idiot savants also use the regularity of the calendar to simplify the task. For example, John, a 13-year-old, "successfully memorized a series of base dates, from which he uses the number of days in each month to count either forward or backward to the desired date" (Hoffman, 1971, p. 19). George was even more proficient in using the regularity of the calendar:

George eventually mastered the full range of 400 years. As the 400-year-cycle is constant, he can connect any day and date by substracting multiples of 400; he is aware of the subpatterns within the 400-year-cycle. (Horwitz, Deming, and Winter, 1969, p. 414)

In other words, idiot savants seem to have evolved systems or rules for application to the calender. Their extensive knowlege of days and dates apparently reflects effective combination of these rules with reference dates within a particular year or series of years.

It is interesting to compare the use of strategies by idiot savants and by normal children. Both groups of

children solve memory problems through the successful combination of strategies and knowledge
from the child's long-term memory. The difference
between the normal child and the idiot savant in this
realm is that the normal child's use of strategies is
characterized by much greater flexibility, so that
strategies are tailored to fit the task at hand. The idiot
savant, in comparison, seems to be rather rigid and
inflexible, in that he develops a strategy for a specific
task and does not use that strategy or other strategies
in other situations. That is, the strategies developed
by idiot savants can *only* apply to a specific domain of
knowledge. They are specific to content.

Several factors that are common to the case his-
tories of many idiot savants are important when considering possible causes of the development of the
idiot savant's ability. In each case, the retarded cognitive development of the child was evident early,
almost always by age 5. Consequently, when the children showed signs of intellectual curiosity through
their interest in numbers, dates, and the like, their
teachers and parents encouraged and fostered this
interest. For example, Rubin and Monaghan (1965, p.
481) described one of these children in this way:

The teacher became aware of how exceptional this ability
was, and he provided her with encouragement. R then
began to gain satisfaction and relief from the frustrations of
schoolwork by letting her visitors know of her ability by
shouting out "I'm a calendar girl." R thoroughly enjoyed
the attention she received when asked to demonstrate this
ability.

From such case reports, there is little doubt that the
attention and the concomitant social reinforcement
received by the child is probably instrumental in the

development of the exceptional abilities. Unfortunately, beyond this general statement we can say very little about the specific factors that contribute to the emergence of exceptional skills in idiot savants.

Summary

Memory was examined in three groups of retarded children. The first group, mildly retarded children, is typified by memory deficits similar to those of young school-age children. The retarded child does not use strategies spontaneously but can be trained to do so. Such instruction may produce lasting change in the trained behavior but rarely produces generalization and rarely elevates the performance of the retarded child to the level of his nonretarded peer. Such generalization seems to depend on the retarded individual's understanding of the workings of a strategy.

The second group of retarded children consisted of the profoundly retarded. Only recently have their memory skills been studied, using the habituation procedures derived to study infants' memory. Profoundly retarded children can recognize stimuli immediately after they have seen them, but not after brief delays.

The third group consisted of idiot savants. These individuals often have exceptional memory skills that can be linked to an extensively practiced strategy and well-developed knowledge within a highly circumscribed domain.

7

Mechanisms of Memory Development

The frog starts life as a small, swimming organism capable only of a fishlike mode of life in the water. It breathes by means of gills, feeds on water plants and pond debris and is equipped with a swimming apparatus in the form of a long tail. . . . The first sign of change comes when buds near the rear end of the animal's trunk begin to develop into limbs: the jumping legs of the frog. . . . In this phase, called prometamorphosis, the animal remains a water-dweller. When the hind legs have grown to about the size of the animal's torso, the tadpole abruptly enters the stage of rapid changes called the metamorphic climax. Forelegs suddenly erupt through small openings in the covering of the gills; the mouth widens and develops powerful jaws and a large tongue; the lungs and skin complete their transformation; nostrils and a mechanism for pumping air develop, and the gills and tail are resorbed by a process of self-digestion and thus disappear. Before the week of climax is over the animal emerges to a new life on land. (Etkin, 1966, p. 76)

This account of the growth of the frog provides a novel perspective on the work I have described on the development of memory from birth to young adulthood. One task of the biologist who is interested in frogs is to describe how the various systems of the body function at each stage in the frog's development. So, for example, biologists may contrast intake of oxygen in tadpoles (via gills) and the adult frog (with lungs). In much the same way, in the previous chapters, we have traced the functioning of several components of memory through different stages of human development.

For the biologist, the more complex question about development in frogs or any other species is *why* these changes occur. What mechanism triggers the emergence of the hind legs in prometamorphosis? What initiates the transformation of the mouth? Why do the lungs and nostrils always emerge before the gills are resorbed and not after? In much the same way, the challenging question for all developmental psychologists is to explain the underlying forces that orchestrate psychological development. As children grow, they achieve ever greater cognitive prowess. What underlying mechanism or set of mechanisms is responsible for this steady march towards mature intellectual and mnemonic power?

In this final chapter we will provide some tentative answers to this question. The fact that only one chapter is devoted to the issue of the mechanism of development is indicative of the stage of the art: Developmental psychologists know much more about differences in the mnemonic skills of older and younger children than they do about the processes that lead young children to acquire greater mnemonic competence. The first part of the chapter concerns the role of *processing resources* as a mechanism underlying memory development. The second part deals with *environmental influences* on the growth of human memory.

Processing Resources

There are severe constraints on the amount of mental activity that a person can conduct at any one time. For example, adolescents learning to drive a car are usually encouraged not to converse with passengers. This advice is based on the realization that driving a car can tax limited processing resources to such an extent that other, unnecessary processing should be minimized. Consistent with this advice, adults remember much more poorly when driving a car than when not (e.g., Zeitlin and Finkelman, 1975). Similarly, when adults simultaneously deal cards and remember words, their recall is poorer than when they perform the memory task by itself, particularly if they are dealing cards into four piles based on suits, instead of into two piles based on colors (Murdock, 1965).

A number of different terms have been used to describe this limit on mental activity, including *limited processing resources*, *limited mental effort*, *the span of awareness*, and *memory span*. Common to all of these terms, however, is the idea that performance on most intellectual tasks takes some mental resources and that all individuals are limited in the resources they can allocate to a task.

Developmental Increases in Processing Resources

As children develop they are capable of performing more complicated cognitive tasks—those that are presumably more taxing in terms of the resources needed for performance. One appealingly simple explanation for this change would be that the total pool of intellectual resources increases as children grow older. McLaughlin (1963), for example, argued that " . . .a subject solving an intellectual problem must retain a number of items at the same time, the number depending on the logical complexity of the problem; and . . . the number of items a child can retain simultaneously increases as he grows older; therefore, as the child matures, he can solve more complex problems" (p. 62).

Regrettably, McLaughlin (1963) did not test his theory experimentally, and for that reason it has had relatively little impact. Nevertheless, it is worthwhile to pursue the rationale behind the theory, using the following purely hypothetical example. Suppose that simple rote rehearsal (e.g., "9-0-8-9-0-8- . . . .") requires 100 units of processing resources and that elaborative rehearsal (e.g., "9-0-8 is my birthdate . . .") takes 150 units. If 4-, 9-, and 14-year-olds have 75, 125, and 175 processing units available, respectively, this would explain the developmental sequence in rehearsal skills that was described in Chapter 2. Either form of rehearsal is too taxing for 4-year-olds; both require more than the 75 processing units available at this age. The 9-year-olds have sufficient resources for rote rehearsal but not elaborative rehearsal; only 14-year-olds have the resources necessary to rehearse elaboratively.

To give this purely hypothetical example some substance, we need to be able to quantify a person's mental resources as well as the demands that a cognitive task places on those resources. Pascual-Leone did just this in a theory first presented in 1969 that has since been modified. He proposed that " . . .the size of central computing space M . . . increases in a lawful manner during normal development" (1970,

p. 304). This central computing space is analogous to our assumption that only a limited quantity of resources is available for thought.

Pascual-Leone (1970) defined M space as $e + k$. The first quantity, e, is the amount of space set aside to store general information about how to perform the task. The k refers to the amount of space set aside for storing information from the task and specific procedures for solving the task. The value of e is thought to be invariant developmentally. That is, at different ages the instructions and general task information occupy the same amount of M space. However, k is thought to increase in discrete steps that are linked directly to a child's chronological age. As depicted in Table 7-1, Pascual-Leone (1970) suggested that k increases by one unit every other year between 3 and 16 years of age.

According to this theory, then, children sometimes fail to use a particular memory strategy because the resources required to use the strategy exceed the child's available M space. Returning to the previous

Table 7-1 M Values at Different Developmental Levels

Age (years)	M Value
3–4	$e + 1$
5–6	$e + 2$
7–8	$e + 3$
9–10	$e + 4$
11–12	$e + 5$
13–14	$e + 6$
15–16	$e + 7$

Note: The value of e is constant across age and refers to the processing capacity necessary for storing the task instructions and a general strategy for solving the task. (Table derived from Case, 1972b.)

example regarding rote and elaborative rehearsal, we can speculate that rote rehearsal exceeds the two available M units for 5- and 6-year-olds, so they cannot use the strategy. By 7 or 8 years of age, M has increased to e + 3, allowing children to rehearse in a rote manner, but not elaboratively.

To test the theory rigorously, we need a task in which the informational demands can be varied systematically. Then the theory can be used to predict those conditions in which children of a particular age should succeed, as well as those conditions in which they should fail. Pascual-Leone and his colleagues have done this in a number of experiments (Pascual-Leone, 1970; Case, 1972a,b; Case and Serlin, 1979; Scardamalia, 1977). An experiment by Case (1972b) is illustrative. Children were shown a series of digits. Their task was to place the last digit in the appropriate place in the series. Shown 3, 8, and 12, they would be asked to place a 10 in the appropriate location between the 8 and 12. Several practice trials of this sort were given until children had mastered the basics of the task. Then the procedure was modified slightly so that each digit was shown individually for approximately one to two seconds. After the last digit was shown, children indicated where it would go in the series.

The 6-, 8-, and 10-year-olds in this experiment were first tested on series where the number of digits presented was equal to the value of k hypothesized for their age. Thus, 6-year-olds saw two digits; 8- and 10-year-olds saw three and four digits, respectively.* Children were then tested on other problems in which the number of digits presented was k + 1:

*The number of digits always includes the final digit, i.e., the digit to be placed. For 6-year-olds, then, the first problems consisted of presentation of a 5, then a 7, with the objective to place the 7 to the right of the 5.

three, four, and five digits were shown to 6-, 8-, and 10-year-olds, respectively.

The general predictions of Pascual-Leone's (1970) theory are straightforward: When the number of digits equals k, all children should solve problems successfully, for available M space equals the quantity of information (i.e., digits) to be remembered. The situation is more complex when the number of digits exceeds k by 1. One digit will be forgotten, and Case (1972b) assumed that all $k + 1$ digits were equally likely to be forgotten. Hence, sometimes the digits that are remembered will be sufficient for a child to answer correctly: Shown 3, 9, and 18 and asked to place the 11, forgetting the 3 should not impair performance. If, instead, the 11 itself were forgotten, the child would simply have to guess, and thus would select the correct location of the four possible locations on 25 percent of the trials. By examining in this manner the predicted consequences on performance of forgetting each of the individual digits in each problem, it is possible to predict the number of problems that a child will solve correctly when the number of digits is greater than the hypothetically available M space.

The number of problems children solved correctly was very close to the number predicted by the k values. For example, if 8-year-olds' M space is $e + 3$, analysis like the one just described leads to a prediction that these children will solve approximately 78 percent of the problems when $n = 5$. In fact, they solved approximately 79 percent accurately. Thus, Case's (1972b) data, like those of other investigators (e.g., Burtis, 1982; Scardamalia, 1977), seem to provide convincing support for Pascual-Leone's (1970) proposed increases in processing capacity, increases that would explain why children are capable of systematically more complex mnemonic acts as they develop (see Halford, 1982, for a related theory).

There is a final important word of caution. The validity of Pascual-Leone's theory depends, in large part, on the accuracy with which we assess the demands of different intellectual tasks. To do so, a number of simplifying assumptions must be made to derive the quantitative predictions. One of these was mentioned earlier, namely, that each of the $k + 1$ digits is equally likely to be forgotten. To the extent that this and other simplifying assumptions are incorrect, the data may be misleading (for a discussion of this issue see Trabasso and Foellinger, 1978; Pascual-Leone, 1978; Trabasso, 1978; Pascual-Leone and Sparkman, 1980).

Automatization and Increases in Functional Capacity

An efficiently run company typically produces more goods from the same amount of resources than does an inefficient company. The same could well be true with intellectual development: An individual who uses resources efficiently may be able to solve more complex tasks than another person with the same resources who uses them less efficiently. This is the crux of another potential mechanism for intellectual development. Specifically, we assume that the total pool of intellectual resources *does not* change as children develop but remains constant. Instead, the developmental mechanism is *automatization*.

Recall that earlier we spoke of the advice frequently given to beginning drivers to concentrate on driving and not to converse or listen to the radio. Few experienced drivers heed these same warnings; indeed most experienced drivers routinely chat or listen to the radio while driving. The difference between the novice and experienced driver is that as greater experience in driving (or sewing, swimming, hitting a baseball) is gained, less capacity is required to perform the task, and thus concurrent processing is allowed. That is, people can do two or more things at once, and do so proficiently, as long as the individual processes are simple enough or sufficiently mastered so that the combined demands of the different processes do not exceed the available processing resources. With sufficient practice, a skill may even be performed *automatically;* that is, it makes no demonstrable demands on processing resources.

Spelke, Hirst, and Neisser (1976) traced the automatization of one such cognitive skill. Two adults were asked to read a story and, at the same time, take dictation. During the first few hours of dictation, they read much more slowly than usual, at about 70 percent of their normal rates. After ten hours of practice they read at approximately 80 percent of their usual rates. Between 20 and 30 hours of practice were needed until these subjects could take dictation and simultaneously read at their normal speeds. In other words, 30 hours of practice seemed to be sufficient to reduce the capacity demands of dictation to the point where the combined demands of reading and dictation no longer exceeded the limits of activated memory.

Ordinarily months or even years of practice are needed for cognitive processes to operate automatically. It is this long period needed to achieve automaticity that makes it a potential developmental variable. In this view, as children grow older they are gradually improving a host of cognitive skills. Each increment in efficiency means that a task will require fewer resources to complete. For example, suppose a cognitive task involves three major processes for solution. Let us assume, first, that the total pool of processing resources is fixed throughout development, and second, that individuals become increasingly proficient at each of the required processes. As depicted in Table 7-2, the result would be that the total resources of the task exceed those available in 4-year-olds; they fail to solve the task. Both 8- and 12-year-olds have sufficient resources to solve the task. Note, however, that 12-year-olds have resources "to spare" which might result in their solving the task more rapidly than 8-year-olds.

An experiment by Guttentag (1984, Experiment 1) can be used to illustrate the automaticity hypothesis more carefully and to contrast it with the hypothesis of developmental increases in total processing resources. Guttentag had 7-, 8-, and 11-year-olds tap a telegraph key as rapidly as possible. On some trials they only tapped; on other trials they tapped and simultaneously used a cumulative rehearsal strategy (see Chapter 2) to learn a list of words: They rehearsed

Table 7-2 *Illustrative Developmental Changes in Processing Efficiency*

	Demands of Three Processes			
Age (years)	A	B	C	Total Demands
4	4	4	3	11
8	3	2	1	6
12	2	1	1	4

Note: In this example, assume that total processing capacity is 6 units at each age.

"each new word as it was presented along with at least two other words presented earlier in the list" (p. 95). At all ages, tapping was slower when done in conjunction with cumulative rehearsal than when tapping was the sole task. However, this effect was greater for younger children. That is, compared to 11-year-olds, 7- and 8-year-olds seemed less able to respond to the joint demands of tapping and rehearsal.

An explanation of this finding in terms of developmental increases in total processing resources might proceed as follows. According to Pascual-Leone, 7-year-olds' available capacity (i.e., k) is 3 but 11-year-olds' is 5. Let us assume that, alone, tapping and cumulative rehearsal each requires 3 processing units. Their *joint* demands would be 6. This value is considerably beyond the 7-year-olds' capacity of 3 but only slightly beyond the 11-year-olds' capacity of 5, which would explain why the younger children have particular difficulty performing the two tasks concurrently.

In explaining the Guttentag (1984, Experiment 1) results in terms of greater processing efficiency with development, we assume that total processing capacity is constant throughout childhood, but that older children, by virtue of greater practice, require fewer resources to perform the tasks individually. Assume that capacity is fixed at 4 units. If the 7-year-olds need 4 units to perform each task individually (i.e., tapping or rehearsing), then the demands of the tasks when performed concurrently amount to 8, far exceeding the available 4 units. We assume that 11-year-olds are more skilled at tapping and rehearsing: Tapping demands 2 units and rehearsing, 3 units. The joint demands of the tasks, 5, exceed available capacity only slightly, which accounts for older children's greater success in performing the tasks concurrently.

Obviously, if we are to take these hypotheses seriously, we cannot simply decide the processing demands of a task on an ad hoc basis. As we discussed earlier, one approach to this problem is to start with a set of assumptions about the nature of processing, then derive the needed processing demands of a task (Pascual-Leone, 1970, 1978). A different approach is illustrated in work by Birch (1978). In her experiment, subjects performed two tasks separately as well as concurrently. The novel aspect of her work is that young children practiced the individual tasks until they acquired older individuals' proficiency on each task. A "tracking" task resembled a video game in that children turned a knob to align a target with a dot that was moving horizontally. In the other task, pairs of words were presented aloud (e.g., *dog, cat; shirt, pants; horse, cap*) and the individual judged if the words belonged to the same conceptual category.

Some 8-year-olds received considerable practice on the tracking and category-judgment tasks. Specifically, they continued practicing until they reached 13-year-olds' level of proficiency, a feat that took between 4 and 15 sessions of practice. These 8-year-olds then performed the tasks concurrently *for the first time* in the experiment.

The logic behind this experiment is sufficiently general that it does not require that we assign precise values to the various quantities as before. Let us simply assume that after the 8-year-olds have achieved the proficiency of 13-year-olds, the joint demands of the tasks for both groups are represented by $a + b$, where a and b refer to the demands of the two tasks. Now, if capacity, k, does not change developmentally, then joint performance should decline by the same amount for the two groups: $a + b > k$ describes the relation between processing demands and processing resources for both groups. If capacity is greater for 13- than 8-year-olds, such that $k_{13} > k_8$, then concurrent performance should decline to a greater extent for 8- than for 13-year-olds.

In fact, after extensive training, 8-year-olds' performance on the tasks concurrently was exactly like that of 13-year-olds. Based on the rationale just outlined, this would appear to provide convincing evidence that processing resources do *not* increase with development. What prevents us from drawing this conclusion is the following: Neither group's performance declined when the two tasks were performed concurrently (compared to when the tasks were performed separately). For both groups, the joint demands, $a + b$, were *less* instead of greater than k. This result is problematic: The 13-year-olds' processing resources could be greater than those of 8-year-olds, $k_{13} > k_8 > a + b$, or the two groups could have equal processing resources, $k_{13} = k_8 > a + b$. In short, we cannot distinguish the two hypotheses of interest.

Approaches like this have been used by a number of investigators to understand age-related changes in processing efficiency and automatization (e.g., Ceci, 1983; Chi, 1977; Hiscock and Kinsbourne, 1978; Kail, 1983; Roth, 1983). We will not consider these experiments in detail for, like the Birch (1978) study, none of these studies provides totally persuasive evidence that would allow us to choose between the hypotheses that (1) the total pool of processing resources increases systematically with age in a manner like that proposed by Pascual-Leone (1970, 1978), or (2) processing capacity is fixed. One firm conclusion from these studies (e.g., Chi, 1977) is that processing efficiency does increase with development. Whether resources are fixed or increase with age, older individuals use those resources more effectively. This fact leads to an important point. We have discussed the two hypotheses as if they were mutually exclusive alternatives. This is not the case. Processing capacity and automaticity may well *both* increase with age; older children's widespread cognitive advantage over young children could be due to the combined effects of having more processing resources available and using those greater resources more efficiently (Kail and Bisanz, 1982).

These two sources of developmental change do differ in a subtle but noteworthy way. Increases in M power represent a fundamental change in the child's mental apparatus. The increased resources represented by an increment in k should be apparent in performance on *any* resource-demanding task. Developmental increases in automatization and processing efficiency do not represent the same pervasive type of change. Instead, they occur only for specific skills that individuals practice extensively. Hence, age differences are not expected on all resource-demanding tasks. If younger and older children use equally efficient strategies (or, for that matter, equally inefficient strategies), then equal performance is expected. Age differences in performance are predicted only for tasks in which older children use more efficient processing strategies.

Environmental Influences

Experience is necessary for children and adults to acquire expertise in most intellectual, social, and physical skills. Children typically achieve competence through sustained interactions with animate and inanimate stimuli in their environments. In understanding children's acquisition of these skills, one of the key issues is to determine those experiences that are essential for the development of skills. In teaching children to read, should their experiences emphasize "sounding out" letters of a word, or should they concentrate on recognizing entire words? Do children learn to ride a bicycle sooner if they use training wheels, or can training wheels be abandoned altogether?

Similar sorts of questions can be asked of the development of memory. What experiences—if any—are necessary for the emergence of the memory skills discussed in earlier chapters? Are there "critical periods" for these experiences (Hunt, 1979), i.e., particular ages at which experiences are especially influential? Progress has been made in answering these questions for the development of mnemonic strategies and we will examine this work in detail.

Schooling and Memory Strategies

In chapter 3, I suggested that use of strategies evolves gradually as part of larger changes in which children begin to identify the goals in cognitive tasks, to frame potential paths to those goals, and to monitor their progress towards the goals. Hagen (1971) proposed that these changes might occur because the child

begins to realize that he is an actor in his environment as well as a reactor to it. Task demands are made increasingly upon him and more differentiated responses are required. What he is really learning is that *he* himself determines how well he does, and that he can improve his performance if he uses certain of his new skills in certain task situations. (pp. 267–268)

In other words, as children grow older, they begin to detect regularities between their behavior and their success in solving memory problems.

The intriguing problem, of course, is to identify those experiences that are essential in order for the child to notice these regularities. Some psychologists, notably Cole and Scribner (1977), believe that experience in formal educational settings may be a key prerequisite for the development of mnemonic strategies.

Schools represent the major cultural institution in technological societies where remembering as a distinct activity, occurring apart from the application of anything remembered, is engaged in repeatedly with a great variety of stimulus materials. . . . It is difficult to think of any other generally experienced setting in which members of technological societies engage in deliberate memorizing. . . . When we turn to societies that lack formal educational institutions, where can we find such activities? The answer, we believe, is rarely. (Cole and Scribner, 1977, p. 269)

In other words, Cole and Scribner (1977) believe that schools are unique in their vigorous emphasis on memorization per se as a behavioral goal and that it is in response to this emphasis that children apparently acquire "general purpose" mnemonic strategies.*

Evaluating this hypothesis is complicated because we need to compare use of strategies by children who attend school versus those who do not attend school. Obviously, amount of education is not a variable that can be manipulated in any short-term

---

*Cole and Scribner (1977) are not claiming individuals living in societies without formal schools are incapable of using all memory strategies. To the contrary, in such societies there are often complicated strategies to enable individuals to remember events and information that are important to the culture. However, these strategies are explicitly tied to specific events and information; they are not "general purpose" like most of the strategies discussed in Chapter 2.

experiment; instead, we must look for situations in which other conditions have dictated that children have limited or no formal education. Because almost all North American and European children attend school from age 6 until adolescence, the research is conducted in parts of the world where formal education is not widespread. Wagner (1974), for example, examined use of rehearsal by individuals living in the Yucatán peninsula of southern Mexico. Some subjects lived in Mérida, the capital city of Yucatán, where nearly all children attend elementary and secondary schools. Another group of subjects lived in Mayapán; here education was limited to grades 1 to 4. In Mérida, rehearsal was infrequent among 7-year-olds but developed gradually from that age on. In Mayapán, there was no evidence of rehearsal in subjects ranging in age from 8 to 27 years. In short, the developmental pattern described in Chapter 2 was seen among individuals attending school regularly but was completely absent among individuals with minimal schooling.

These results seem to fit nicely with Cole and Scribner's (1977) predictions about the necessity of schooling for the onset of strategies. However, we must consider a potential problem before we can accept Wagner's (1974) results with confidence. Compulsory, universal schooling usually is associated with a host of other cultural changes that may cloud our interpretation of schooling as the determinant of differences in strategic behavior. The two communities in Wagner's (1974) study differed along a number of dimensions that might be important. Mérida has many features of a modern city—radio and television, theaters, and a university. Mayapán, in contrast, has no electricity or running water and was (in 1973) accessible primarily by foot or on horseback. Perhaps one of these variables, or some combination of them, is responsible for the differences in memory performance.

Wagner (1978) addressed this issue in a subsequent experiment conducted in Morocco. Here schooled and unschooled individuals were identified in both rural and urban areas. Among the individuals who attended school, rehearsal skill developed gradually between the ages of 7 and 19, in both rural and urban settings. In contrast, for individuals with minimal schooling, rehearsal was infrequent at all ages. In this study, then, as in the previous experiment (Wagner, 1974), the findings point to schooling as a necessary ingredient in the acquisition of strategic skill.

Why Does Schooling Have Impact?

The evidence certainly points to a link between schooling and the development of strategies. But it is prudent to be extremely cautious in making conclusions based on cross-cultural comparisons. Such a link need not occur via the mechanism proposed by Cole and Scribner (1977). Several alternatives are plausible (Rogoff, 1981a).

Selection Bias. A key assumption in Wagner's (1974, 1978) work is that educated and uneducated children are alike *prior* to their attendance at school. Only if this is true can differences in performance be attributed to schooling. This assumption need not be true; one can envision a number of situations in which educated and uneducated children differ prior to their entry into school. Children may not attend school because their parents (1) are too poor to send them; (2) do not value formal education; or (3) think their child is not bright enough to profit from instruction. That is, of the 5- or 6-year-olds in a country, those who attend school may be a select and distinctly nonrandom sample.

Hence, we need to determine the reasons why children do (or do not) attend school in these cultures. Sharp, Cole, and Lave (1979, Chapter 5) examined three general factors that might determine how many years of education an adult received in Yucatán: (1) the amount of education available in the person's town; (2) the person's intellectual ability; and (3) the degree to which the person's attendance in school represented an economic hardship for the family.* Of these, the amount of education available in the town best predicted the amount of an individual's education. Measures of a person's intellectual skills, such as IQ or the person's native language, were related to the extent of schooling, but only modestly. Hence, Sharp, Cole, and Lave (1979) concluded "that the level of one's education in Yucatán is in large measure determined by economic and cultural factors over which the individual has relatively little control and that intellectual test-performance differences among our populations are best attributed to differences in education and work experience" (1979, pp. 72–73).

Rogoff (1981b) reached much the same conclusion in a study conducted in Guatemala. She looked at the relationship between memory performance and a variety of variables, including the amount of a child's schooling and such familial variables as

---

*Schooling is an economic burden because of the costs of books and clothing for the student. Also, attendance at school means losing income that the student would have provided otherwise (Sharp, Cole, and Lave, 1979).

occupation, wealth, and parent's education. Only the child's amount of schooling was consistently related to memory performance.

Familiarity with Testing. Testing is an important and frequent ritual in formal schools. Perhaps this familiarity with testing—due to its similarity to the testing involved in psychological experimentation—may explain the differences observed in strategic behavior. Maybe unschooled individuals simply fail to use strategies because they are unfamiliar with or intimidated by the laboratory setting. If this hypothesis is correct, then uneducated individuals should perform poorly on *all* memory tasks, not just on those that require the use of strategies. That is, unfamiliarity and intimidation point to a pervasive deficit in memory performance.

In fact, Wagner (1978) also tested Moroccans on a recognition memory task that minimized the need for strategies. Here differences in retention between literate and illiterate individuals were completely eliminated for those living in rural areas and were reduced greatly among urban residents. Thus, the findings described earlier are not simply due to the schoolchild's greater awareness of and ease with laboratory-like tasks and settings.

Search for General Rules. If differences in memory strategies between schooled and unschooled children are not due to selection biases or greater familiarity with testing, then the key factor is probably associated with the instruction that goes on in schools. In fact, there is very little research on the memory demands of routine instruction and how children respond to those demands. However, as Rogoff (1981a) has noted, many theorists have "proposed that schooling emphasizes the use of explicitly stated rules, and that schoolchildren are taught to look for rules from which specific instances can be understood" (p. 276).

This search for general rules certainly characterizes much instruction in mathematics, science, and expository writing. What may also occur is that children search for the same rules in the multitude of tests they experience in school. From specific tests in different school subjects, children may derive general rules about properties of tests and test-relevant behavior. In short, the argument linking schooling to use of memory strategies involves two parts. The first is that schools are unique in their emphasis on deliberate remembering, as manifested by frequent testing of school material. The second is that from this frequent testing, children abstract certain general principles of tests and test-taking.

One implication of this argument is that not all types of schooling should lead to the use of strategies. Schools where testing is infrequent or unchanging in format should not promote the development of strategies. An interesting test of this prediction is provided in Wagner's (1978) study. He tested a sample of adults attending a Koranic school where individuals spend most of their time memorizing passages from the Koran, the sacred book of Islam. According to Wagner, "Methods of memorizing appeared to involve writing special notes or commentaries next to certain passages, and vocal rehearsal of passages. This latter method was sometimes accompanied by changing tonalities in chanting that appeared to mark segments of the passage being memorized" (1978, p. 7). In fact, the Koranic students showed no evidence of rehearsal on Wagner's experimental task. One explanation of this surprising result is that Koranic students never have the opportunity to learn the *general* value of strategies like rehearsal because their remembering occurs exclusively in the single context of memorizing the Koran.

This evidence fits with the explanation of the link between schooling and strategies, but the claim remains quite speculative, for as we noted earlier, there is very little research on memory demands in actual school settings. Nevertheless, one facet of this explanation warrants attention, for it addresses the larger issue of environmental influences on cognitive development generally. Schooling is like other global demographic variables such as social class and race that are often linked to equally global psychological variables like intelligence or memory. Middle-class children are said to be more intelligent than lower-class children; educated children remember more accurately than uneducated children. The problem here is that social class and schooling refer to such heterogeneous entities that they have little explanatory value per se. Schooling, for example, does not refer to a single experience but to a potpourri of cognitive, social, and physical experiences. Furthermore, these experiences vary among schools as well as among individuals within the same school. Of course, much the same can be said of memory: One of the major themes of this book is that memory is a diverse and heterogeneous collection of cognitive skills. Notice that the argument linking schooling to memory is framed in terms of specific components of schooling and specific aspects of memory. The specificity of this argument is an important asset, for most environmental influences seem to operate in this way. As Wachs and Gruen (1982) concluded after reviewing evidence on the impact of experience on intellectual development, "The majority of environmental parameters will be specific to particular abilities, particular ages, or particular classes of individuals" (p. 200).

A Concluding Remark about Schooling and Strategies

We have discussed the link between schooling and strategies at length simply because it represents one intersection of environment and cognition that has been studied with enough care so that conclusions can be drawn with some confidence. The length should not imply that schooling is the sole childhood experience of import, nor should it imply that strategies represent the only aspect of memory that can be modified by experience. School-age children routinely remember routes to friends' homes, to playgrounds, and to schools; they remember the rules to games and scores of games; they remember promises made by parents and teachers. All of these represent familiar experiences for school-age children in which retention is a key component. Even preschool children have experiences that shape the growth of memory. Parents certainly place memory demands on their children, chiefly in the form of remembering certain routines, like brushing one's teeth (Wellman and Somerville, 1980). How these and other experiences outside of school influence the growth of memory is simply unknown.

Environmental Influences and Processing Resources

The impact of experience certainly depends on the changes in processing resources that were discussed in the first part of this chapter. Actually, this linkage refers to the well-known—but poorly understood— concepts of *readiness* and *critical periods* (Hunt,

1979; Spear, 1984; Wachs and Gruen, 1982). "Critical periods refer to time periods when . . . the organism is particularly sensitive to environmental stimulation" (Wachs and Gruen, 1982, p. 194). Readiness refers to a child's entry into such a critical period, or, more generally, a time when a child can profit from experiences that were ineffectual previously.

Central to both concepts is the idea that children are sometimes unable to profit from experience. One explanation of this phenomenon would be limited processing resources that are insufficient for the information-processing demands of an experience. Illustratively, if a particular experience has M power demands of 4, based on developmental changes in M power (see Table 7-1), children 9 years and older should profit from the experience but younger children should not. In fact, when younger and older children are taught to use a new memory strategy, older children typically use the new strategy more effectively (e.g., Ornstein, Naus, and Stone, 1977). This may occur because limited processing resources act as a "filter" for memory-relevant experiences; younger children do not profit as much from the training experience because the processing demands of the experience exceed their available resources.

Summary

The underlying mechanisms of growth provided the focus of this chapter. Processing resources, referring to the amount of mental "effort" that a person can devote to a task, might be one such mechanism. Some theorists, notably Pascual-Leone (1970, 1978), have suggested that processing resources increase steadily with development. Supporting this view are experiments in which, based on an evaluation of the processing demands of a task, one successfully predicts the age at which children will solve the task correctly. However, analysis of the processing demands of tasks depends on several key assumptions, some of which may not be justified.

An alternative view is that processing resources are fixed throughout development but that older individuals use those resources more efficiently. Here the relevant experimentation supports the contention of age-related changes in efficiency of processing but is equivocal concerning the presence or absence of change in processing resources.

Environmental influences represent a second important mechanism for change. Most of the research concerns the impact of attending school. There is convincing evidence that schooling facilitates children's acquisition of strategies and that the findings related to schooling are not due to selection biases or to the children's greater ease with laboratory experiments. Rather, the relationship apparently stems from the fact that schools emphasize retention as an explicit goal and provide students with diverse test-like experiences.

Finally, it was emphasized that limited processing resources may explain why there are "critical periods" in development, that is, periods in which experiences may be particularly influential.

References

Acredolo, L. P., Pick, H. L., and Olsen, M. G. Environmental differentiation and familiarity as determinants of children's memory for spatial location. *Developmental Psychology*, 1975, *11*, 495–501.

Ainsworth, M. D. S. The development of infant-mother attachment. In B. M. Caldwell and H. N. Ricciuti (Eds.), *Review of child development research*, Vol. 3. Chicago: University of Chicago Press, 1973.

Alberts, J. R. Sensory-perceptual development in the Norway rat: A view towards comparative studies. In R. Kail and N. E. Spear (Eds.), *Comparative perspectives on the development of memory*. Hillsdale, N.J.: Lawrence Erlbaum Associates, 1984.

Anderson, J. R., and Bower, G. H. Recognition and retrieval processes in free recall. *Psychological Review*, 1972, *79*, 97–123.

Appel, L. F., Cooper, R. G., McCarrell, N., Sims-Knight, J., Yussen, S. R., and Flavell, J. H. The development of the distinction between perceiving and memorizing. *Child Development*, 1972, *43*, 1365–1381.

Ashmead, D. H., and Perlmutter, M. Infant memory in everyday life. In M. Perlmutter (Ed.), *New directions for child development*, Vol. 10: Children's memory. San Francisco: Jossey-Bass, 1980.

Aslin, R. N. Sensory and perceptual constraints on memory in human infants. In R. Kail and N. E. Spear (Eds.), *Comparative perspectives on the development of memory*. Hillsdale, N.J.: Lawrence Erlbaum Associates, 1984.

Bahrick, H. P. Two-phase model for prompted recall. *Psychological Review*, 1970, *77*, 215–222.

Bahrick, H. P., Bahrick, P. O., and Wittlinger, R. P. Fifty years of memory for names and faces: A cross-sectional approach. *Journal of Experimental Psychology: General*, 1975, *104*, 54–75.

Bartlett, F. C. *Remembering*. Cambridge, England: Cambridge University Press, 1932.

Belmont, J. M., and Butterfield, E. C. The relation of short-term memory to development and intelligence. In L. Lipsitt and H. Reese (Eds.), *Advances in child development and behavior*, Vol. 4. New York: Academic Press, 1969.

Belmont, J. M., and Butterfield, E. C. Learning strategies as determinants of mental deficiencies. *Cognitive Psychology*, 1971, *2*, 411–420.

Belmont, J. M., and Butterfield, E. C. The instructional approach to cognitive developmental research. In R. V. Kail and J. W. Hagen (Eds.), *Perspectives on the development of memory and cognition*. Hillsdale, N.J.: Lawrence Erlbaum Associates, 1977.

Belmont, J. M., Butterfield, E. C., and Borkowski, J. G. Training retarded people to generalize memory methods across memory tasks. In M. M. Gruneberg, P. E. Morris, and R. N. Sykes (Eds.), *Practical aspects of memory*. New York: Academic Press, 1978.

Birch, L. L. Baseline differences, attention, and age differences in time-sharing performance. *Journal of Experimental Child Psychology*, 1978, *25*, 505–513.

Bisanz, G. L., Vesonder, G. T., and Voss, J. F. Knowledge of one's own responding and the relation of such knowledge to learning: A developmental study. *Journal of Experimental Child Psychology*, 1978, *25*, 116–128.

Borkowski, J. G., and Cavanaugh, J. C. Maintenance and generalization of skills and strategies by the retarded. In N. R. Ellis (Ed.), *Handbook of mental deficiency* (2nd ed.). Hillsdale, N.J.: Lawrence Erlbaum Associates, 1979.

Bower, G. H., Clark, M. C., Lesgold, A. M., and Winzenz, D. Hierarchical retrieval schemes in recall of categorized word lists. *Journal of Verbal Learning and Verbal Behavior*, 1969, *8*, 323–343.

Bower, T. G. R., Broughton, J. M., and Moore, M. K. The development of the object concept as manifested by changes in the tracking behavior of infants between 7 and 20 weeks of age. *Journal of Experimental Child Psychology*, 1971, *11*, 182–193.

Brown, A. L. Context and recency cues in the recognition memory of retarded children and adolescents. *American Journal of Mental Deficiency*, 1972, *77*, 54–58.

Brown, A. L. The role of strategic behavior in retardate memory. In N. R. Ellis (Ed.), *International review of research in mental retardation*, Vol. 7. New York: Academic Press, 1974.

Brown, A. L. The development of memory: Knowing, knowing about knowing, and knowing how to know. In H. W. Reese (Ed.), *Advances in child development and behavior*, Vol. 10. New York: Academic Press, 1975.

Brown, A. L. Knowing when, where, and how to remember: A problem of metacognition. In R. Glaser (Ed.), *Advances in instructional psychology*, Vol. 1. Hillsdale, N.J.: Lawrence Erlbaum Associates, 1978.

Brown, A. L., and Day, J. D. Macrorules for summarizing text: The development of expertise. *Journal of Verbal Learning and Verbal Behavior*, 1983, *22*, 1–14.

Brown, A. L., and Scott, M. S. Recognition memory for pictures in preschool children. *Journal of Experimental Child Psychology*, 1971, *11*, 401–412.

Brown, A. L., and Smiley, S. S. The development of strategies for studying texts. *Child Development*, 1978, *49*, 1076–1088.

Brown, A. L., Bransford, J. D., Ferrara, R. A., and Campione, J. C. Learning, remembering, and understanding. In J. H. Flavell and E. M. Markman (Eds.), *Handbook of child psychology*, Vol. 3. New York: Wiley, 1983.

Brown, A. L., Campione, J. C., and Barclay, C. R. Training self-checking routines for estimating test readiness: Generalization from list learning to prose recall. *Child Development*, 1979, *50*, 501–512.

Brown, A. L., Campione, J. C., and Murphy, M. D. Keeping track of changing variables: Long-term retention of a trained rehearsal strategy by retarded adolescents. *American Journal of Mental Deficiency*, 1974, *78*, 446–453.

Brown, A. L., Campione, J. C., and Murphy, M. D. Maintenance and generalization of trained metamnemonic awareness by educable retarded children. *Journal of Experimental Child Psychology*, 1977, *24*, 191–211.

Brown, A. L., Smiley, S. S., and Lawton, S. Q. C. The effects of experience on the selection of suitable retrieval cues for studying texts. *Child Development*, 1978, *49*, 829–835.

Brown, A. L., Smiley, S. S., Day, J. D., Townsend, M. A. R., and Lawton, S. C. Intrusion of a thematic idea in children's comprehension and retention of stories. *Child Development*, 1977, *48*, 1454–1466.

Brown, R., and Kulik, J. Flashbulb memories. *Cognition*, 1977, *5*, 73–99.

Burger, A. L., Blackman, L. S., and Tan, N. Maintenance and generalization of a sorting and retrieval strategy by EMR and nonretarded individuals. *American Journal of Mental Deficiency*, 1980, *84*, 373–380.

Burtis, P. J. Capacity increase and chunking in the development of short-term memory. *Journal of Experimental Child Psychology*, 1982, *34*, 387–413.

Butcher, M. J. Recognition memory for colors and faces in profoundly retarded young children. *Intelligence*, 1977, 1, 344–357.

Campbell, B. A., and Jaynes, J. Reinstatement. *Psychological Review*, 1966, 73, 478–480.

Campbell, B. A., Misanin, J. R., White, B. C., and Lytle, L. D. Species differences in ontogeny of memory: Indirect support for neural maturation as a determinant of forgetting. *Journal of Comparative and Physiological Psychology*, 1974, 87, 193–202.

Campione, J. C., and Brown, A. L. Memory and metamemory development in educable retarded children. In R. V. Kail and J. W. Hagen (Eds.), *Perspectives on the development of memory and cognition*. Hillsdale, N.J.: Lawrence Erlbaum Associates, 1977.

Carter, P., and Strauss, M. S. Habituation is not enough, but it's not a bad start—A reply to Sophian. *Merrill-Palmer Quarterly*, 1981, 27, 333–337.

Case, R. Learning and development: A neo-Piagetian interpretation. *Human Development*, 1972a, 15, 339–358.

Case, R. Validation of a neo-Piagetian mental capacity construct. *Journal of Experimental Child Psychology*, 1972b, 14, 287–302.

Case, R., and Serlin, R. A new processing model for predicting performance on Pascual-Leone's test of M-space. *Cognitive Psychology*, 1979, 11, 308–326.

Ceci, S. J. Automatic and purposive semantic processing characteristics of normal and language/learning-disabled children. *Developmental Psychology*, 1983, *19*, 427–439.

Ceci, S. J., Caves, R. D., and Howe, M. J. A. Children's long-term memory for information that is incongruous with their prior knowledge. *British Journal of Psychology*, 1981, *72*, 443–450.

Chi, M. T. H. Age differences in memory span. *Journal of Experimental Child Psychology*, 1977, *23*, 266–281.

Chi, M. T. H. Knowledge structures and memory development. In R. Siegler (Ed.), *Children's thinking: What develops?* Hillsdale, N.J.: Lawrence Erlbaum Associates, 1978.

Cohen, L. B., and Gelber, E. R. Infant visual memory. In L. B. Cohen and P. Salapatek (Eds.), *Infant perception: From sensation to cognition*, Vol. 1. New York: Academic Press, 1975.

Cole, M., and Scribner, S. Cross-cultural studies of memory and cognition. In R. V. Kail and J. W. Hagen (Eds.), *Perspectives on the development of memory and cognition*. Hillsdale, N.J.: Lawrence Erlbaum Associates, 1977.

Cornell, E. H. Infants' recognition memory, forgetting, and savings. *Journal of Experimental Child Psychology*, 1979, *28*, 359–374.

Coulter, X. The determinants of infantile amnesia. In N. E. Spear and B. A. Campbell (Eds.), *Ontogeny of learning and memory*. Hillsdale, N.J.: Lawrence Erlbaum Associates, 1979.

Cultice, J. C., Somerville, S. C., and Wellman, H. M. Preschoolers' memory monitoring: Feeling of knowing judgments. *Child Development*, 1983, *54*, 1480–1486.

Cuvo, A. J. Incentive level influence on overt rehearsal and free recall as a function of age. *Journal of Experimental Child Psychology*, 1974, *18*, 167–181.

Cuvo, A. J. Developmental differences in rehearsal and free recall. *Journal of Experimental Child Psychology*, 1975, *19*, 265–278.

Daehler, M., Bukatko, D., Benson, K., and Myers, N. The effects of size and color cues on the delayed response of very young children. *Bulletin of the Psychonomic Society*, 1976, *7*, 65–68.

Davis, J. M, and Rovee-Collier, C. K. Alleviated forgetting of a learned contingency in 8-week-old infants. *Developmental Psychology*, 1983, *19*, 353–365.

DeCasper, A. J., and Fifer, W. P. Of human bonding: Newborns prefer their mothers' voices. *Science*, 1980, *208*, 1174–1176.

DeLoache, J. S., and Brown, A. L. Looking for Big Bird: Studies of memory in very young children. *Quarterly Newsletter of the Laboratory of Comparative Human Cognition*, 1979, *1*, 53–57.

DeLoache, J. S., and Brown, A. L. Very young children's memory for the location of objects in a large scale environment. *Child Development*, 1983, *54*, 888–897.

Dempster, F. N. Memory span: Sources of individual and developmental differences. *Psychological Bulletin*, 1981, *89*, 63–100.

Dudycha, G. J., and Dudycha, M. M. Some factors and

characteristics of childhood memories. *Child Development*, 1933, *4*, 265–278.

Dugas, J. L., and Kellas, G. Encoding and retrieval processes in normal children and retarded adolescents. *Journal of Experimental Child Psychology*, 1974, *17*, 177–185.

Duncan, E. M., Whitney, P., and Kunen, S. Integration of visual and verbal information in children's memories. *Child Development*, 1982, *53*, 1215–1223.

Ellis, N. R. The stimulus trace and behavioral inadequacy. In N. R. Ellis (Ed.), *Handbook of mental deficiency*. New York: McGraw-Hill, 1963.

Ellis, N. R. (Ed.), *Handbook of mental deficiency* (2nd. ed). Hillsdale, N.J.: Lawrence Erlbaum Associates, 1979.

Ellis, N. R., McCartney, J. R., Ferretti, R. P., and Cavalier, A. R. Recognition memory in mentally retarded persons. *Intelligence*, 1977, *1*, 310–317.

Ericsson, K. A., Chase, W. G., and Faloon, S. Acquisition of a memory skill. *Science*, 1980, *208*, 1181–1182.

Etkin, W. How a tadpole becomes a frog. *Scientific American*, 1966, *214*(5), 76–88.

Fagan, J. F. Memory in the infant. *Journal of Experimental Child Psychology*, 1970, *9*, 217–226.

Fagan, J. F. Infants' delayed recognition memory and forgetting. *Journal of Experimental Child Psychology*, 1973, *16*, 424–450.

Fagen, J. W., and Rovee-Collier, C. K. A conditioning analysis of infant memory: How do we know they know what we know they knew? In R. L. Isaacson and N. E. Spear (Eds.), *The expression of knowledge.* New York: Plenum, 1982.

Fantz, R. L., Fagan, J. F., and Miranda, S. B. Early visual selectivity. In L. B. Cohen and P. Salapatek (Eds.), *Infant perception: From sensation to cognition,* Vol. 1. New York: Academic Press, 1975.

Feigley, D. A., and Spear, N. E. Effect of age and punishment condition on long-term retention by the rat of active- and passive-avoidance learning. *Journal of Comparative and Physiological Psychology,* 1970, *73,* 515–526.

Ferguson, R. P., and Bray, N. W. Component processes of an overt rehearsal strategy in young children. *Journal of Experimental Child Psychology,* 1976, *21,* 490–506.

Flavell, J. H. *The developmental psychology of Jean Piaget.* New York: Van Nostrand, 1963.

Flavell, J. H. Developmental studies of mediated memory. In H. W. Reese and L. P. Lipsitt (Eds.), *Advances in child development and behavior,* Vol. 5. New York: Academic Press, 1970.

Flavell, J. H. First discussant's comments: What is memory development the development of? *Human Development,* 1971, *14,* 272–278.

Flavell, J. H. Metacognition and cognitive monitoring: A new area of cognitive-developmental inquiry. *American Psychologist,* 1979, *34,* 906–911.

Flavell, J. H., and Wellman, H. M. Metamemory. In R. V. Kail and J. W. Hagen (Eds.), *Perspectives on* the development of memory and cognition. Hillsdale, N.J.: Lawrence Erlbaum Associates, 1977.

Flavell, J. H., Beach, D. R., and Chinsky, J. M. Spontaneous verbal rehearsal in a memory task as a function of age. Child Development, 1966, 37, 283–299.

Flavell, J. H., Friedrichs, A. G., and Hoyt, J. D. Developmental changes in memorization processes. Cognitive Psychology, 1970, 1, 324–340.

Fox, N., Kagan, J., and Weiskopf, S. The growth of memory during infancy. Genetic Psychology Monographs, 1979, 99, 91–130.

Freud, S. Three essays on the theory of sexuality. In J. Strachey (Ed.), The standard edition of the complete psychological works of Sigmund Freud, Vol. 7. London: Hogarth, 1953. (Originally published, 1905).

Friedman, S. Habituation and recovery of visual response in the alert human newborn. Journal of Experimental Child Psychology, 1972a, 13, 339–349.

Friedman, S. Newborn visual attention to repeated exposure of redundant vs. "novel" targets. Perception & Psychophysics, 1972b, 12, 291–294.

Friedman, S., Bruno, L. A., and Vietze, P. Newborn habituation to visual stimuli: A sex difference in novelty detection. Journal of Experimental Child Psychology, 1974, 18, 242–251.

Gelabert, T., Torgesen, J., Dice, C., and Murphy, H. The effects of situational variables on the use of rehearsal by first-grade children. Child Development, 1980, 51, 902–905.

Glidden, L. M. Developmental effects in free recall learning. *Child Development*, 1977, *48*, 9–12.

Gold, E., and Neisser, U. Recollections of kindergarten. *Quarterly Newsletter of the Laboratory of Comparative Human Cognition*, 1980, *2*, 77–80.

Goodman, C., and Gardiner, J. M. How well do children remember what they have recalled? *British Journal of Educational Psychology*, 1981, *51*, 97–101.

Gottlieb, G. Ontogenesis of sensory function in birds and mammals. In E. Tobach, L. R. Aronson, and E. Shaw (Eds.), *The biopsychology of development*. New York: Academic Press, 1971.

Guttentag, R. E. The mental effort requirement of cumulative rehearsal: A developmental study. *Journal of Experimental Child Psychology*, 1984, *37*, 92–106.

Haake, R. J., Somerville, S. C., and Wellman, H. M. Logical ability of young children in searching a large-scale environment. *Child Development*, 1980, *51*, 1299–1302.

Hagen, J. W. Some thoughts on how children learn to remember. *Human Development*, 1971, *14*, 262–271.

Halford, G. S. *The development of thought*. Hillsdale, N.J.: Lawrence Erlbaum Associates, 1982.

Hall, J. W., Murphy, J., Humphreys, M. S., and Wilson, K. P. Children's cued recall: Developmental differences in retrieval operations. *Journal of Experimental Child Psychology*, 1979, *27*, 501–511.

Haroutunian, V., and Riccio, D. C. Drug-induced "arousal" and the effectiveness of CS exposure in the reinstatement of memory. *Behavioral and Neural Biology*, 1979, *26*, 115–120.

Harris, G. J., and Fleer, R. E. High speed memory scanning in mental retardates: Evidence for a central processing deficit. *Journal of Experimental Child Psychology*, 1974, *17*, 452–459.

Harris, P. L., Mandias, F., Terwogt, M. M., and Tjintjelaar, J. The influence of context on story recall and feelings of comprehension. *International Journal of Behavioral Development*, 1980, *3*, 159–172.

Hayes-Roth, B., and Hayes-Roth, F. Concept learning and the recognition and classification of exemplars. *Journal of Verbal Learning and Verbal Behavior*, 1977, *16*, 321–338.

Hill, A. L. Savants: Mentally retarded individuals with special skills. In N. R. Ellis (Ed.), *International Review of Research in Mental Retardation*, Vol. 9. New York: Academic Press, 1978.

Hiscock, M., and Kinsbourne, M. Ontogeny of cerebral dominance: Evidence from time-sharing asymmetry in children. *Developmental Psychology*, 1978, *14*, 321–329.

Hoffman, E. The idiot savant: A case report and a review of explanations. *Mental Retardation*, 1971, *9*, 18–21.

Horwitz, W. A., Deming, W. E., and Winter, R. F. A further account of the idiots savants, experts with the calendar. *American Journal of Psychiatry*, 1969, *126*, 412–415.

Hunt, J. McV. Psychological development: Early experience. *Annual Review of Psychology,* 1979, *30,* 104–143.

Hunter, W. S. The delayed reaction in animals and children. *Behavior Monographs,* 1913, *2,* 1–86.

Hunter, W. S. The delayed reaction in a child. *Psychological Review,* 1917, *24,* 74–87.

Inhelder, B. Memory and intelligence in the child. In D. Elkind and J. Flavell (Eds.), *Studies in cognitive development.* New York: Oxford University Press, 1969.

Jensen, A. R., and Rohwer, W. D. The effects of verbal mediation on the learning and retention of paired associates by retarded adults. *American Journal of Mental Deficiency,* 1963, *68,* 80–84.

Johnson, C. N., and Wellman, H. M. Children's developing understanding of mental verbs: Remember, know, and guess. *Child Development,* 1980, *51,* 1095–1102.

Jones, B. F., and Hall, J. W. School applications of the mnemonic keyword method as a study strategy by eighth graders. *Journal of Educational Psychology,* 1982, *74,* 230–237.

Jones, H. E. Phenomenal memorizing as a "special ability." *Journal of Applied Psychology,* 1926, *10,* 367–377.

Kagan, J., Klein, R. E., Finley, G. E., Rogoff, B., and Nolan, E. A cross-cultural study of cognitive development. *Monographs of the Society for Research in Child Development,* 1979, *44,* Whole No. 180.

Kail, R. RS: A case study in the acquisition of spatial

skill. Presented at the annual meeting of the Merrill-Palmer Society, 1983.

Kail, R., and Bisanz, J. Information processing and cognitive development. In H. W. Reese (Ed.), *Advances in child development and behavior*, Vol. 17. New York: Academic Press, 1982.

Kail, R. V., and Hagen, J. W. (Eds.), *Perspectives on the development of memory and cognition*. Hillsdale, N.J.: Lawrence Erlbaum Associates, 1977.

Kail, R. V., and Levine, L. E. Encoding processes and sex-role preferences. *Journal of Experimental Child Psychology*, 1976, *21*, 256–263.

Keeney, T. J., Cannizzo, S. R., and Flavell, J. H. Spontaneous and induced verbal rehearsal in a recall task. *Child Development*, 1967, *38*, 953–966.

Kendall, C. R., Borkowski, J. G., and Cavanaugh, J. C. Metamemory and the transfer of an interrogative strategy by EMR children. *Intelligence*, 1980, *4*, 255–270.

Keniston, A. H., and Flavell, J. H. A developmental study of intelligent retrieval. *Child Development*, 1979, *50*, 1144–1152.

Kennedy, R. F. *Times to remember*. Garden City, N.Y.: Doubleday, 1974.

Kobasigawa, A. Utilization of retrieval cues by children in recall. *Child Development*, 1974, *45*, 127–134.

Koblinsky, S., and Cruse, D. F. The role of frameworks in children's retention of sex-related story content. *Journal of Experimental Child Psychology*, 1981, *31*, 321–331.

Koblinsky, S., Cruse, D. F., and Sugawara, A. I. Sex-role stereotypes and children's memory for story content. *Child Development*, 1978, 49, 452–458.

Kramer, J. J., and Engle, R. W. Teaching awareness of strategic behavior in combination with strategy training: Effects on children's memory performance. *Journal of Experimental Child Psychology*, 1981, 32, 513–530.

Kreutzer, M. A., Leonard, C., and Flavell, J. H. An interview study of children's knowledge about memory. *Monographs of the Society for Research in Child Development*, 1975, 40 (1, Serial No. 159), 1–58.

Landis, T. Y. Interactions between text and prior knowledge in children's memory for prose. *Child Development*, 1982, 53, 811–814.

Levin, J. R., Pressley, M., McCormick, C. B., Miller, G. E., and Shriberg, L. K. Assessing the classroom potential of the keyword method. *Journal of Educational Psychology*, 1979, 71, 583–594.

Liben, L. S. Evidence for developmental differences in spontaneous seriation and its implication for past research on long-term memory improvement. *Developmental Psychology*, 1975a, 11, 121–125.

Liben, L. S. Long-term memory for pictures related to seriation, horizontality, and verticality concepts. *Developmental Psychology*, 1975b, 11, 795–806.

Liben, L. S. Memory from a cognitive-developmental perspective: A theoretical and empirical review. In W. Overton and J. Gallagher (Eds.), *Knowledge and development*, Vol. 1. New York: Plenum Press, 1977a.

Liben, L. S. Memory in the context of cognitive development: The Piagetian approach. In R. V. Kail and J. W. Hagen (Eds.), *Perspectives on the development of memory and cognition.* Hillsdale, N.J.: Lawrence Erlbaum Associates, 1977b.

Liben, L. S., and Posnansky, C. J. Inferences on inferences: The effects of age, transitive ability, memory load, and lexical factors. *Child Development,* 1977, *48*, 1490–1497.

Lindsay, P. H., and Norman, D. A. *Human information processing: An introduction to psychology.* New York: Academic Press, 1972.

Lodico, M. G., Ghatala, E. S., Levin, J. R., Pressley, M., and Bell, J. A. The effects of strategy-monitoring training on children's selection of memory strategies. *Journal of Experimental Child Psychology,* 1983, *35*, 263–277.

McCall, R. B., Parke, R. D., and Kavanaugh, R. D. Imitation of live and televised models by children one to three years of age. *Monographs of the Society for Research in Child Development,* 1977, *42*, Whole No. 173.

McLaughlin, G. H. Psycho-logic: A possible alternative to Piaget's formulation. *British Journal of Educational Psychology,* 1963, *33*, 61–67.

Mandler, J. M., and Robinson, C. A. Developmental changes in picture recognition. *Journal of Experimental Child Psychology,* 1978, *26*, 122–136.

Markman, E. Factors affecting the young child's ability to monitor his memory. Unpublished doctoral dissertation, University of Pennsylvania, 1973.

Martin, C. L., and Halverson, C. F. The effects of

sex-typing on young children's memory. *Child Development*, 1983, *53*, 563–574.

Martin, R. M. Effects of familiar and complex stimuli on infant attention. *Developmental Psychology*, 1975, *11*, 178–185.

Masur, E. F., McIntyre, C. W., and Flavell, J. H. Developmental changes in apportionment of study time among items in a multitrial free recall task. *Journal of Experimental Child Psychology*, 1973, *15*, 237–246.

Maurer, D., Siegel, L. S., Lewis, T. L., Kristofferson, M. W., Barnes, R. A., and Levy, B. A. Long-term memory improvement? *Child Development*, 1979, *50*, 106–118.

Moely, B. E., Olson, F. A., Halwes, T. G., and Flavell, J. H. Production deficiency in young children's clustered recall. *Developmental Psychology*, 1969, *1*, 26–34.

Moynahan, E. D. The development of knowledge concerning the effect of categorization upon free recall. *Child Development*, 1973, *44*, 238–246.

Moynahan, E. D. Assessment and selection of paired associate strategies: A developmental study. *Journal of Experimental Child Psychology*, 1978, *26*, 257–266.

Murdock, B. B. Effect of a subsidiary task on short-term memory. *British Journal of Psychology*, 1965, *56*, 413–419.

Myers, M., and Paris, S. G. Children's metacognitive knowledge about reading. *Journal of Educational Psychology*, 1978, *70*, 680–690.

Nicholls, J. G. The development of the concepts of

effort and ability, perception of academic attainment, and the understanding that difficult tasks require more ability. *Child Development*, 1978, *49*, 800–814.

Olson, G. M., and Sherman, T. Attention, learning, and memory in infants. In M. M. Haith and J. Campos (Eds.), *Handbook of child psychology*, Vol. 2. New York: Wiley, 1983.

Olson, G. M., and Strauss, M. S. The development of infant memory. In M. Moscovitch (Ed.), *Infant memory*. New York: Plenum, 1984.

Ornstein, P. A. (Ed.), *Memory development in children*. Hillsdale, N.J.: Lawrence Erlbaum Associates, 1978.

Ornstein, P. A., Naus, M. J., and Liberty, C. Rehearsal and organizational processes in children's memory. *Child Development*, 1975, *46*, 818–830.

Ornstein, P. A., Naus, M. J., and Stone, B. P. Rehearsal training and developmental differences in memory. *Developmental Psychology*, 1977, *13*, 15–24.

O'Sullivan, J. T., and Pressley, M. Completeness of instruction and strategy transfer. *Journal of Experimental Child Psychology*, 1984, in press.

Paris, S. G. Coordination of means and goals in the development of mnemonic skills. In P. A. Ornstein (Ed.), *Memory development in children*. Hillsdale, N.J.: Lawrence Erlbaum Associates, 1978.

Paris, S. G., and Carter, A. Y. Semantic and constructive aspects of sentence memory in children. *Developmental Psychology*, 1973, *9*, 109–113.

Paris, S. G., and Cross, D. R. Ordinary learning: Pragmatic connections among children's beliefs, motives, and actions. In J. Bisanz, G. Bisanz, and R. Kail (Eds.), *Learning in children: Progress in cognitive development research.* New York: Springer-Verlag, 1983.

Paris, S. G., and Lindauer, B. K. The role of inference in children's comprehension and memory for sentences. *Cognitive Psychology,* 1976, 8, 217–227

Paris, S. G., and Mahoney, G. J. Cognitive integration in children's memory for sentences and pictures. *Child Development,* 1974, 45, 633–642.

Paris, S. G., Lindauer, B. K., and Cox, G. L. The development of inferential comprehension. *Child Development,* 1977, 48, 1728–1733.

Paris, S. G., Newman, R. S., and McVey, K. A. Learning the functional significance of mnemonic actions: A microgenetic study of strategy acquisition. *Journal of Experimental Child Psychology,* 1982, 34, 490–509.

Pascual-Leone, J. A mathematical model for the transition rule in Piaget's developmental stages. *Acta Psychologica,* 1970, 32, 301–345.

Pascual-Leone, J. Compounds, confounds, and models in developmental information processing: A reply to Trabasso and Foellinger. *Journal of Experimental Child Psychology,* 1978, 26, 18–40.

Pascual-Leone, J., and Sparkman, E. The dialectics of empiricism and rationalism: A last methodological reply to Trabasso. *Journal of Experimental Child Psychology,* 1980, 29, 88–101.

Perlmutter, M. (Ed.), *New directions for child development*, Vol. 10: Children's memory. San Francisco: Jossey-Bass, 1980.

Pezdek, K. Life-span differences in semantic integration of pictures and sentences in memory. *Child Development*, 1980, 51, 720–729.

Pezdek, K., and Miceli, L. Life-span differences in memory integration as a function of processing time. *Developmental Psychology*, 1982, 18, 485–490.

Piaget, J. *The child's conception of number.* New York: Humanities Press, 1952.

Piaget, J., and Inhelder, B. *Memory and intelligence.* New York: Basic Books, 1973.

Potash, M., and Ferguson, H. B. The effect of criterion level on the acquisition and retention of a one-way avoidance response in young and old rats. *Developmental Psychobiology*, 1977, 10, 347–354.

Pressley, M., Borkowski, J. G., and O'Sullivan, J. T. Memory strategy instruction is made of this: Metamemory and durable strategy use. *Educational Psychologist*, 1984, in press.

Pressley, M., and Dennis-Rounds, J. Transfer of a mnemonic keyword strategy at two age levels. *Journal of Educational Psychology*, 1980, 72, 575–582.

Pressley, M., and Levin, J. R. Developmental constraints associated with children's use of the keyword method of foreign language vocabulary learning. *Journal of Experimental Child Psychology*, 1978, 26, 359–372.

Pressley, M., and Levin, J. R. (Eds.), *Cognitive strategy research: Psychological Foundations.* New York: Springer-Verlag, 1983.

Pressley, M., Levin, J. R., and Ghatala, E. S. Memory-strategy monitoring in adults and children. *Journal of Verbal Learning and Verbal Behavior,* 1984, *23,* 270–288.

Richardson, R., Ebner, D. L., and Riccio, D. C. Effects of delayed testing on passive avoidance of conditioned fear stimuli in young rats. *Bulletin of the Psychonomic Society,* 1981, *18,* 211.

Rogoff, B. Schooling and the development of cognitive skills. In H. C. Triandis and A. Heron (Eds.), *Handbook of cross-cultural psychology,* Vol. 4.: Developmental Psychology. Boston: Allyn & Bacon, 1981a.

Rogoff, B. Schooling's influence on memory test performance. *Child Development,* 1981b, *52,* 260–267.

Rogoff, B., Newcombe, N., and Kagan, J. Planfulness and recognition memory. *Child Development,* 1974, *45,* 972–977.

Roth, C. Factors affecting developmental changes in the speed of processing. *Journal of Experimental Child Psychology,* 1983, *35,* 509–528.

Rovee-Collier, C. The ontogeny of learning and memory in human infancy. In R. Kail and N. E. Spear (Eds.), *Comparative perspectives on the development of memory.* Hillsdale, N.J.: Lawrence Erlbaum Associates, 1984.

Rovee-Collier, C. K., and Fagen, J. W. The retrieval of memory in early infancy. In L. P. Lipsitt and C. K.

Rovee-Collier (Eds.), *Advances in infancy research*, Vol. 1. Norwood, N.J.: Ablex, 1981.

Rovee-Collier, C. K., Sullivan, M. W., Enright, M., Lucas, D., and Fagen, J. Reactivation of infant memory. *Science*, 1980, *208*, 1159–1161.

Rubin, E. J., and Monaghan, S. Calendar calculation in a multiple-handicapped blind person. *American Journal of Mental Deficiency*, 1965, *70*, 478–485.

Scardamalia, M. Information processing capacity and the problem of horizontal décalage: A demonstration using combinatorial reasoning tasks. *Child Development*, 1977, *48*, 28–37.

Scheerer, M., Rothman, E., and Goldstein, K. A case of "idiot savant": An experimental study of personality organization. *Psychological Monographs*, 1945, *58*(4), 1–63.

Sharp, D., Cole, M., and Lave, C. Education and cognitive development: The evidence from experimental research. *Monographs of the Society for Research in Child Development*, 1979, *44*, Whole No. 178.

Sheingold, K., and Tenney, Y. J. Memory for a salient childhood event. In U. Neisser (Ed.), *Memory observed: Remembering in natural contexts*. San Francisco: W. H. Freeman, 1982.

Shepherd, P. A., and Fagan, J. F. Visual pattern detection and recognition memory in children with profound mental retardation. In N. R. Ellis (Ed.), *International Review of Research in Mental Retardation*, Vol. 10. New York: Academic Press, 1981.

Shriberg, L. K., Levin, J. R., McCormick, C. B., and Pressley, M. Learning about "famous" people via the keyword method. *Journal of Educational Psychology*, 1982, *74*, 238–247.

Slater, A., Morison, V., and Rose, D. Visual memory at birth. *British Journal of Psychology*, 1982, *73*, 519–525.

Small, M. Y, and Butterworth, J. Semantic integration and the development of memory for logical inferences. *Child Development*, 1981, *52*, 732–735.

Smith, G. J., and Spear, N. E. Role of proactive interference in infantile forgetting. *Animal Learning and Behavior*, 1981, *9*, 371–380.

Sophian, C. Habituation is not enough: Novelty preferences, search, and memory in infancy. *Merrill-Palmer Quarterly*, 1980, *26*, 239–257.

Sophian, C. Reply: Habituation may not be a bad start, but it's time to expand our horizons. *Merrill-Palmer Quarterly*, 1981, *27*, 339–344.

Spear, N. E. Experimental analysis of infantile amnesia. In J. F. Kihlstrom and F. J. Evans (Eds.), *Functional disorders of memory*. Hillsdale, N.J.: Lawrence Erlbaum Associates, 1979.

Spear, N. E. Ecologically determined dispositions control the ontogeny of learning and memory. In R. Kail and N. E. Spear (Eds.), *Comparative perspectives on the development of memory*. Hillsdale, N.J.: Lawrence Erlbaum Associates, 1984.

Spear, N. E., and Kucharski, D. Ontogenetic differences in stimulus selection during conditioning. In R. Kail and N. E. Spear (Eds.), *Comparative perspectives on the development of memory.* Hillsdale, N.J.: Lawrence Erlbaum Associates, 1984.

Speer, J. R., and Flavell, J. H. Young children's knowledge of the relative difficulty of recognition and recall memory tasks. *Developmental Psychology,* 1979, *15,* 214–217.

Spelke, E., Hirst, W., and Neisser, U. Skills of divided attention. *Cognition,* 1976, *4,* 215–230.

Spitz, H. H. The role of input organization in the learning and memory of mental retardates. In N. R. Ellis (Ed.), *International review of research in mental retardation,* Vol. 2. New York: Academic Press, 1966.

Sternberg, S. High-speed scanning in human memory. *Science,* 1966, *153,* 652–654.

Strauss, M. S. Abstraction of prototypical information by adults and 10-month-old infants. *Journal of Experimental Psychology: Human Learning and Memory,* 1979, *5,* 618–632.

Strauss, M. S., and Carter, P. Infant memory: Limitations and future directions. In R. Kail and N. E. Spear (Eds.), *Comparative perspectives on the development of memory.* Hillsdale, N.J.: Lawrence Erlbaum Associates, 1984.

Strauss, M. S., and Cohen, L. B. Infant immediate and delayed memory for perceptual dimensions. Presented at the International Conference on Infant Studies, 1980.

Sullivan, M. W. Reactivation: Priming forgotten memories in human infants. *Child Development,* 1982, *53,* 516–523.

Tomkins, S. S. A theory of memory. In J. S. Antrobus (Ed.), *Cognition and affect.* Boston: Little, Brown, 1970.

Trabasso, T. On the estimation of parameters and the evaluation of a mathematical model: A reply to Pascual-Leone. *Journal of Experimental Child Psychology,* 1978, *26,* 41–45.

Trabasso, T., and Foellinger, D. B. Information processing capacity in children: A test of Pascual-Leone's model. *Journal of Experimental Child Psychology,* 1978, *26,* 1–17.

Tulving, E., and Thomson, D. M. Encoding specificity and retrieval processes in episodic memory. *Psychological Review,* 1973, *80,* 352–373.

Wachs, T. D., and Gruen, G. E. *Early experience and human development.* New York: Plenum, 1982.

Wagner, D. A. The development of short-term and incidental memory: A cross-cultural study. *Child Development,* 1974, *45,* 389–396.

Wagner, D. A. Memories of Morocco: The influence of age, schooling, and environment on memory. *Cognitive Psychology,* 1978, *10,* 1–28.

Wagner, D. A. Culture and memory development. In H. C. Triandis and A. Heron (Eds.), *Handbook of cross-cultural psychology,* Vol. 4.: Developmental Psychology. Boston: Allyn and Bacon, 1981.

Waldfogel, S. The frequency and affective character of childhood memories. *Psychological Monograph,* 1948, *62,* Whole No. 291.

Wellman, H. M. The early development of intentional memory behavior. *Human Development,* 1977a, *20,* 86–101.

Wellman, H. M. Preschoolers' understanding of memory-relevant variables. *Child Development*, 1977b, 48, 1720–1723.

Wellman, H. M. Tip of the tongue and feeling of knowing experiences: A developmental study of memory-monitoring. *Child Development*, 1977c, 48, 13–21.

Wellman, H. M. Knowledge of the interaction of memory variables: A developmental study of metamemory. *Developmental Psychology*, 1978, 14, 24–29.

Wellman, H. M. Metamemory revisited. In M. T. H. Chi (Ed.), *Contributions to human development*, Vol. 9: Trends in memory development research. Basel: S. Karger, 1983.

Wellman, H. M., and Johnson, C. N. Understanding of mental processes: A developmental study of "remember" and "forget". *Child Development*, 1979, 50, 79–88.

Wellman, H. M., and Somerville, S. C. Quasi-naturalistic tasks in the study of cognition: The memory-related skills of toddlers. In M. Perlmutter (Ed.), *New directions for child development*, Vol. 10: Children's memory. San Francisco: Jossey-Bass, 1980.

Wellman, H. M., Collins, J., and Glieberman, J. Understanding the combination of memory variables: Developing conceptions of memory limitations. *Child Development*, 1981, 52, 1313–1317.

Wellman, H. M., Ritter, K., and Flavell, J. H. Deliberate memory behavior in the delayed reactions of very young children. *Developmental Psychology*, 1975, *11*, 780–787.

Wellman, H. M., Somerville, S. C., and Haake, R. J. Development of search procedures in real-life spatial environments. *Developmental Psychology*, 1979, *15*, 530–542.

Werner, J. S., and Perlmutter, M. Development of visual memory in infants. In H. W. Reese and L. P. Lipsitt (Eds.), *Advances in child development and behavior*, Vol. 14. New York: Academic Press, 1979.

Wertheimer, M. Psycho-motor coordination of auditory-visual space at birth. *Science*, 1961, *134*, 1692.

White, S. H., and Pillemer, D. B. Childhood amnesia and the development of a socially accessible memory system. In J. F. Kihlstrom and F. J. Evans (Eds.), *Functional disorders of memory*. Hillsdale, N.J.: Lawrence Erlbaum Associates, 1979.

Yussen, S. R. Determinants of visual attention and recall in observational learning by preschoolers and second graders. *Developmental Psychology*, 1974, *10*, 93–100.

Yussen, S. R., and Bird, J. E. The development of metacognitive awareness in memory, communication, and attention. *Journal of Experimental Child Psychology*, 1979, *28*, 300–313.

Yussen, S. R., and Levy, V. M. Developmental changes in predicting one's own span of short-term memory. *Journal of Experimental Child Psychology*, 1975, *19*, 502–508.

Zeitlin, L. R., and Finkelman, J. M. Subsidiary techniques of digit generation and digit recall as indirect measures of operator loading. *Human Factors*, 1975, *17*, 218–220.

Zigler, E. Developmental versus difference theories of mental retardation and the problem of motivation. *American Journal of Mental Deficiency*, 1969, *73*, 536–556.

Author Index

205

Subject Index